Getting Them to Talk:
A Guide to Leading Discussions
in Middle Grades Classrooms

Susan Edwards

Association for Middle Level Education
Westerville, Ohio

Printed in the United States of America.

ISBN: 978-1-56090-266-9

Library of Congress Cataloging-in-Publication Data

Edwards, Susan, 1975-
Getting them to talk : a guide to leading discussions in middle grades classrooms / Susan Edwards.
    pages cm
ISBN 978-1-56090-266-9
1. Oral communication--Study and teaching (Middle school) 2. Discussion--Study and teaching (Middle school) 3. Listening--Study and teaching (Middle school) I. Title.
    LB1572.E38 2014
    372.62'2--dc23
                            2014005011

Association for Middle Level Education
4151 Executive Parkway, Suite 300
Westerville, Ohio 43081 | www.amle.org

To Steve, my wonderful husband, who cheers me on
and believes in me no matter what.

Table of Contents

Introduction

You may have picked up this book because you believe strongly in getting students to discuss ideas in class, or perhaps you are feeling pressure from the Common Core Standards to support students in developing their discussion skills. Whether you have been leading class discussions for years and you are seeking new ideas for your repertoire or you are a new teacher who is a little uncomfortable with the idea of having to respond to whatever direction your wily middle school students take the conversation, my goal is to support your work.

Confession: I have not always been comfortable with class discussions and have had more than one unfortunate lesson in which the talk was, well, let's just say, not on topic. You know those professional development videos of perfect teaching moments, with students eagerly raising their hands anxious to contribute deep and insightful ideas to the discussion? Those were never filmed in my classroom.

However, I am one of those people who learns from my mistakes and learns from others. Because the research and my experience show that students learn through social interaction, I was motivated to figure out how to successfully lead class discussions. I began asking other people what they did and how they did it. I attended sessions at professional conferences on the topic and I did a lot of reflection. A lot. I found that planning a structure for class discussions improved them, and I began collecting the strategies that I share in this book. I have gotten better and better at facilitating discussions over the years and am now more convinced than ever that students need to talk about what they are learning and that they learn through that talk.

Let's get real about what happens when you tell a room full of middle level students to talk. They do. The trick is to get them talking in a purposeful way. Though I can't give you a magic formula for keeping your students on target, I share in this book workable strategies I have collected over many years that will engage your students in conversations about your content. I also hope you will feel empowered to use that natural inclination middle level students have to talk with each other as leverage to get them to engage with your content at a deeper level.

Chapter 1
Value of Talk at the Middle Level

Why is talk important for learning? It helps us articulate what we know and believe and gives us the chance to try out different ideas to see if they have credibility under scrutiny from others. If we can learn to listen to others and really hear their arguments, we can then reflect on how they coincide with our own thinking and beliefs and refine our own thinking.

The challenge for middle grades teachers is: In our subject areas, with our content standards, how can we best help our students move from the concrete thinking of their elementary days to an ever-increasing analytical, complex way of thinking? How will we develop their thinking and communicating with others so that they become successful adults capable of thoughtful contributions to their communities at large?

The adolescent brain is developing in areas of reasoning/problem solving, decision making/hypothetical situations, processing information/efficiency, expertise/use of experience, and moral reasoning/social cognition. Our challenge is to support and encourage our students in all these areas so that they can reach their goals. Is it easy? No. Is it doable? Yes.

This book will show you how to create questions that help students in their intellectual development. It will provide strategies, background, and advice on the mechanics of class discussions that could open up the world to them—the world as others think about it and experience it. Discussions allow them to develop empathy and intellectual depth, and as they learn to share, they find out that they are not alone in their journey through adolescence.

Before we get to strategies for encouraging productive student talk, let us first discuss the reasons for making this a priority. First, research on adolescent development shows that middle grades students learn best through social interaction and active learning. Second, the strength of our democracy lies in its citizens having the ability to productively engage in civil discourse. Third, we know that the future employers of our present middle schoolers highly prioritize communication and collaboration skills. And fourth, the standards require it. Let's discuss each of these reasons in a little more depth.

Developmentally Appropriate

Sandra Schurr (2003) offers these reasons for the importance of class discussions in middle level classrooms:

1. They provide the teacher with feedback about student learning.
2. They lend themselves to higher order thinking skills.
3. They help students develop interests and values as well as change attitudes.
4. They allow students to become more active participants in their learning.
5. They enable students to hear and offer alternative points of view and to explore complex issues. (p. 26)

Identity formation.

As educators, we can't overestimate the effect that class discussions can have on young adolescents' identity development. Middle schoolers, in forming their identities, must try out ideas and try on different personas in the process of figuring out how they as individuals link to society and as they link their childhoods to their adulthoods. All the ways they interact with others in small and large groups impact who they become: whether they speak or hold back in groups, whether they agree or disagree with the majority view, whether they hold onto their position or change it due to peer pressure, whether others really listen to them or the teacher dismisses them as "off topic" before really understanding how they are linking their ideas together.

> Young adolescents "negotiate" their views of themselves—how competent they can be, how independent they can be, how well they can get along with others—in their interactions with other people. Over time, in the "give and take" of these interactions, they form a stronger sense of identity or reinforce beliefs of inadequacy. (Strahan, L'Esperance, Van Hoose, 2009, p. 67)

Social interaction.

If you have spent 2 minutes in a classroom full of middle level students, you know that you are working against a force of nature to suppress students' talking. In her study of what types of teaching practices students prefer, Theobald (2003) found that of the 155 seventh graders surveyed, 82% said they either liked or really liked discussions. Why not harness this force for good? Acceptance among their peers is at the forefront of middle grades students' minds. If they are able to navigate those social relationships successfully, they are more likely to turn their attention towards academic work (Brighton, 2007; Strahan, L'Esperance, van Hoose, 2009). Allowing students to talk with each other gives them the opportunity to develop their ability to interact positively with their peers within a structured environment and under the guidance of a teacher.

Social and cognitive connections. Vygosky's studies (1978) of the connection between cognitive development and collaborative activities showed "social interactions—with other children and with adults—enable children to expand their prior knowledge and their use of language...language as a social tool for sharing thoughts and language as a psychological tool for constructing thoughts" (Wood, Roser, & Martinez, 2001). Other studies have shown the significance of dialogue in shaping the way adolescents understand the world and how social learning connections result in products that are far more complex than those constructed individually. Strahan, L'Esperance, and Van Hoose (2009) summarized it:

> When conversation becomes purposeful dialogue, collaboration is more than getting along nicely. It is actively interpreting, processing, and making sense of new information. These dynamics clearly integrate neurological, cognitive, and social modes of reasoning, all of which flow together in learning through experience. (pp. 31–32)

Active learning. Abundant research shows that young adolescents learn best when they are actively engaged in learning as opposed to passively receiving knowledge. When teachers facilitate activities that allow students to take ownership and responsibility for their learning through collaboration with other students and the teacher, learning is greatly enhanced (NMSA, 2010). An additional key characteristic of successful middle level education is for teachers to use multiple learning and teaching approaches, one of which is interaction and dialogue among students and with the teacher. Progressive educators have proposed for over a century that we stimulate students' growth through activities that encourage inquiry, problem solving, creativity, collaboration and self-expression and that teachers should act as facilitators of learning rather than knowledge givers (Gutek, 2004; Schiro, 2008).

Democratic Education

Obviously, our country has difficulty with productive civil discourse as evidenced by the inability of political parties in Congress to reach informed decisions through discussion, critical analysis, and reflection. And TV is rife with talk shows and reality shows of people talking "at" rather than "with" each other. Perhaps if middle school students learn to listen to opposing viewpoints and engage in critical analysis, they will appreciate the necessity of doing so and have the skills to do so as adults. I do not believe early adolescents have an innate ability to consider opposing viewpoints in a civil manner. In fact, the amount of violence in middle schools appears to be evidence that they have difficulty with this, so we must teach them the skills of presenting alternative viewpoints in a constructive manner.

Some suggest that one of the main priorities of schooling should be preparing students to be active participants in our democratic society by critically analyzing and reflecting on topics and issues. An open flow of ideas and the ability to consider the ideas of those who have a different perspective is critical to the discourse necessary in a democracy. Classrooms that prepare students to be engaged citizens encourage a community of learning where all early adolescents consider a range of ideas, engage in discussion and debate, and develop critical thinking skills as they make informed conclusions about problems and ideas (Apple & Beane, 2007; Beane, 2013).

Teachers have the opportunity to use class discussions as a tool not only to teach content, but also to teach the skills necessary to participate in civil discourse. Teachers can guide students to really listen to the ideas of others, to consider ideas intellectually, to look for evidence to support or discredit different claims, to introduce an opposing point of view in a productive way, to analyze data together, and to support their own opinions with evidence.

Employer Demands

Hansen & Hansen (2010) shared a review of 20 skills and values employers look for in job-seekers. Eight of those skills can be directly influenced and developed through class discussions: communication skills, interpersonal abilities, multicultural sensitivity, problem solving, teamwork, adaptability/flexibility, positive attitude, and willingness to learn. When teachers use class discussions as a pedagogical tool, they are helping to prepare their students to be successful in the workforce.

Research shows that people with strong verbal skills have more success both professionally and socially because they can communicate clearly, avoid misunderstandings, and have power in persuading others to adopt their points of view. Those with strong communication skills are simply more impressive to others, both in person, on the phone, and through electronic media.

Comprehension and Collaboration Standards

Forty-five states have adopted the Common Core State Standards (CCSS). The middle grades standards include a focus on speaking, listening, and using textual information to support claims. For example, in grades 6–8 students are asked to, "Engage effectively in a range of collaborative discussions (one-on-one, in groups, and teacher-led) with diverse partners on grade topics, texts, and issues, building on others' ideas and expressing their own clearly" (Common Core State Standards Initiative, 2013, Comprehension and Collaboration Section, para. 1). This book is designed to provide you the tools to help your students meet the comprehension and collaboration standards:

- **CCSS.ELA-Literacy.SL.6-8.1** Engage effectively in a range of collaborative discussions and issues, building on others' ideas and expressing their own clearly.
  - **CCSS.ELA-Literacy.SL.6-8.1a** Come to discussions prepared, having read or studied required material; explicitly draw on that preparation by referring to evidence on the topic, text, or issue to probe and reflect on ideas under discussion.
  - **CCSS.ELA-Literacy.SL.6-8.1b** Follow rules for collegial discussions, set specific goals and deadlines, and define individual roles as needed.
  - **CCSS.ELA-Literacy.SL.6-8.1c** Pose and respond to specific questions with elaboration and detail by making comments that contribute to the topic, text, or issue under discussion.
  - **CCSS.ELA-Literacy.SL.6-8.1d** Review the key ideas expressed and demonstrate understanding of multiple perspectives through reflection and paraphrasing.
  - **CCSS.ELA-Literacy.SL.6-8.2** Interpret information presented in diverse media and formats (e.g., visually, quantitatively, orally) and explain how it contributes to a topic, text, or issue under study.
  - **CCSS.ELA-Literacy.SL.6-8.3** Delineate a speaker's argument and specific claims, distinguishing claims that are supported by reasons and evidence from claims that are not (Common Core State Standards Initiative, 2013, Comprehension and Collaboration Section, para. 1).

Table 1-1 lists the skills students must demonstrate before and during discussions. This book will focus on explicitly teaching these skills and providing strategies for students to actively practice them.

Table 1-1

Before a Discussion
• Read or study material being discussed
• Come prepared with evidence for conclusions
• Understand rules for collegial discussions
• Set goals and deadlines
• Interpret information in diverse media and formats
During a Discussion
• Build on others' ideas
• Express their own ideas clearly
• Refer to evidence
• Probe ideas under discussion
• Reflect on ideas under discussion
• Respond with elaboration and detail
• Understand multiple perspectives
• Paraphrase contributions of others
• Distinguish claims supported by reasons and evidence from those that are not

Chapter 2

Planning Discussions and Creating High Quality Questions

Asking good questions is the best tool in your toolkit. Always.

—Field Guide for Change Agents

Good discussions take careful planning and orchestration. This chapter discusses how to determine the four key parts of productive discussions: the purpose, the key concepts, the question(s), and the structure. Good discussions begin with good questions. Though it is probably not impossible to turn a bad question into a decent discussion, it sure is a lot more difficult. Beginning with a rich question that requires a lot of thinking leads more easily to a productive discussion. The group needs something to mull over, something worth their time and energy, something that is best figured out with others rather than alone.

Planning

Purpose—What is/are the learning objective(s) you want to accomplish with this discussion? What do you hope the students will understand or know by the end? Clearly articulating your purpose will help you assess afterward whether the discussion truly accomplished your objective. I recommend setting a content objective (aligned with your content standards) and a collaboration objective (aligned with the collaboration standards) for discussions. At the beginning of the discussion, emphasize the collaboration objective and how you will assess whether they have met it (what you will look for). Examples of collaboration objectives and assessments for them are:

- Objective: The students will build on the ideas of others. (Look for students adding contributions to others' statements rather than just sharing their prepared thoughts.)

- Objective: The students will express their own ideas with clarity. (Look for thoughtful, clear explanations that everyone can understand.)

- Objective: The students will refer to evidence from the text. (Look for students backing up their statements by referencing statements and examples from the reading.)

- Objective: The students will pose their own questions to further the discussion. (Look for students asking questions about the content rather than only answering teacher questions.)

- Objective: The students will evaluate the soundness of the speakers' reasoning. (Look for students analyzing comments of other students based on evidence from the text or sound reasoning.)

Key Concepts—Identify the key concepts to be discussed. Create an outline that includes terms defined, concepts described, problems, points, or events to be explained (Schurr, 2003). Actually make a list so that you can check them off as they are mentioned in the discussion. Write them on the board when they are brought up. Have students write those ideas in their notes as they arise. If all of the key concepts on your list are not mentioned by students, then you can either prompt students towards those specific ideas, or you can bring them up yourself. See the Key

Concepts list in the Example of a Discussion Plan that follows.

The Question(s)—Before class select and/or write the question(s) you will ask. When trying to think of questions off-the-cuff in front of a class of 30 students, teachers tend to ask low-level questions. Later in this chapter I discuss how to write high-level, thought-provoking questions, but the point here is to do this in advance.

Structure—Chapters 5 and 8 provide many ways to structure discussions involving small groups, whole-class groups, or both; try to use a variety of structures.

A friendly word of advice: Have a plan, but leave some room for students to move the discussion in various directions. The discussion does not have to follow your pre-determined order of key points.

Example of a Discussion Plan

Content Objective—Students will be able to explain the impact of major environmental concerns in Latin America.

Collaboration Objective—Students will be able to respond to the comments of other students and build on those ideas. Students will add to the contributions of others rather than stating their prepared thoughts.

Key Concepts

- Air pollution in Mexico City
- Destruction of the rain forest in Brazil
- Oil-related pollution in Venezuela
- Health problems
- Quality of life issues
- Economic issues

Question—What are the major environmental issues in Latin America, and what is the impact of those issues?

Structure—Numbered Heads Together (see Chapter 8)

To take it a step further, require that students prepare for the discussion. Give them a note-taking sheet to use as they read the selection. Then, during the discussion, when their classmates mention new information, students can add notes to their sheets. Things that might be included on the sheet:

Note-Taking Sheet to Prepare for Discussions

- Facts or statistics that seem important: _____

_____

_____

_____

- Questions that I have: _____

_____

_____

_____

- Terms or concepts to consider: _____

_____

_____

_____

- Personal experiences that relate to this topic: _____

_____

_____

_____

Another method of helping students prepare for a discussion is to have them mark their reading with sticky notes containing their thoughts and questions as they arise. During the discussion later, this helps them recall what they were thinking so they can share it. For a video with examples, see Appendix D.

High Quality Questions

This section begins with an explanation of the types and qualities of questions that have the potential for leading to rich discussions about your content area and includes practical question stems and examples of probing questions that challenge students to go deeper.

Qualities of good discussion questions. Questions that have potential for yielding productive discussions are both divergent and higher order.

1. *Divergent questions* (those with more than one possible correct answer) have more potential than convergent questions (those with one correct answer) for eliciting engaged participants in discussion.

    Example of divergent question: What issues are involved with scientists being able to get accurate measurements from seismographs?

    Example of convergent question: What is a seismograph?

Convergent questions do not work well for discussions because once the correct answer has been determined, well, there is nothing to discuss. Asking convergent questions in your class helps you ensure students have required basic knowledge, but they do not elicit good class discussions.

2. *High-Level questions*—such as those identified by Blooms Taxonomy (Appendix A) as applying, analyzing, and creating—challenge students to think, wrestle with the content, raise doubt, suggest a controversy, encourage students to collaborate and have enough depth that students can work together on figuring them out. Although selecting and writing high-level questions is difficult, there are many good resources with such questions, so you need not create all of them. But

it's critical that you be able to recognize a high-level question. In general, good discussion questions ask students to think more deeply and critically, examine information on their own, analyze, make inferences, synthesize, evaluate, make applications, and solve problems. If a question can be answered without having to pause and think, it is not a high-level question.

Qualities of poor discussion questions. In addition to convergent questions, avoid these types in planning discussions.

1. *Preference questions:* a question whose answer is based solely on an individual's preference. For example, "What is your favorite European country?" does not require compelling evidence to answer correctly, just an opinion ("It's a cool place.")

2. *Questions that are too broad:* questions not aligned to learning objectives will elicit a wide range of answers with no common purpose or focus. For example, "What did you all think about the article?" Student answers might focus on a wide range of issues such as the quality of the writing, whether the topic was appealing or important, the length of the article, whether it had pictures or fuzzy copy that was difficult to read. Ask a question that aligns with the learning objective for the lesson. What content do you want the students to learn? What question will lead students to understanding that content?

3. *Low-level questions:* Low-level questions, such as those on the remember and understand levels of Bloom's Taxonomy (Appendix A) that ask students to simply repeat facts and have a simple, correct answer do not lead to rich class discussions. An indication that you

are focusing on low-level reasoning is finding yourself asking a lot of questions. Less is more. One or two high-level questions are more effective in engaging students to interact with each other and the content.

Examples of low-level questions:
What is the setting of this story?
What is ¾ of 80?
What is the capital of Brazil?
What are the three main groups of protists?

Three categories for framing discussion questions

Three categories for framing discussion questions are (1) How do we make sense of this? (2) What do we think about this? (3) How can we use this? The following section discusses the types of questions that fall in each category.

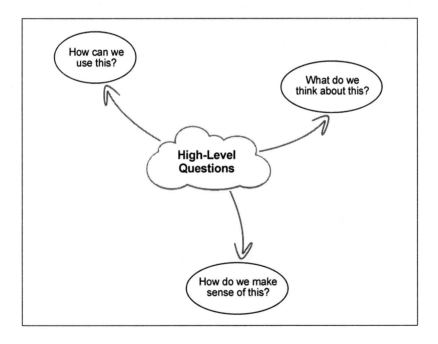

Category 1: How Do We Make Sense of This? Questions that fall into this category require students to examine resources on a particular topic and make sense of it. Students synthesize by putting ideas together in a new way; analyze essential concepts and themes; understand causes, reasons, or methods of what has occurred; compare and contrast ideas; and classify ideas into categories. The following question stems are general examples that could be applied to any content area.

Synthesis
> What are the major themes of the passage?
> I only know about ____. How would you explain ____ to me?
> What would be a good headline or title for this passage?
> Can you state in one sentence what the whole page is about?
> Can you state in 2-3 sentences what the whole story is about?
> Under what conditions is ____ true or not true?
> What conjectures can you make?
> Is there a general rule?
> What are the key points or big ideas in this lesson?

Analysis
> What is the main point of the author's argument? How does he support it?
> What evidence is given to show that ____?
> What are the characteristics of ____?
> What are examples of ____?
> What were the major points of ____ (the chapter, article, book, etc.)?
> How would you explain it in a simpler way?"
> How would you explain this to younger students?
> How could you help someone without giving them the answer?
> Can you explain what you know?
> How can we categorize these ideas?

Compare and Contrast
> What is the connection between ____ and ____?
> How is ____ like ____?
> What is the relationship between ____ and ____?
> How would you compare ____ and ____?
> How would you contrast ____ and ____?
> What do ____ and ____ have in common?
> What is the difference between ____ and ____?

Causes/Results/Process
> What caused ____?
> What are the procedures or processes?
> What is the sequence of events?
> What are the major causes of this situation?
> Why did ____ happen?
> What happened as a result of ____?
> Suppose ____ happened, what would be the consequences?
> What are ways that ____ have impacted ____?

Category 2: What do we think about this? Questions in this category ask students to react to information they have. They require students to do things like make interpretations, make inferences, or evaluate something based on established criteria. The following question stems in this category are general examples that could be applied to any content area.

Interpretation and Inference
> What does the author mean when he says ____?
> How would ____ view this?
> How would this look to a ____?
> How would you feel if you were ____?
> What would ____ mean from the viewpoint of ____?
> Why do you think the author wrote this?
> Can you explain what ____ said in different words?
> What does it mean to say that ____?

Evaluation

Who would you rate as the most skillful _____? Why?

Is there a better solution to _____?

What is the value of _____?

Do you think _____ is a good thing or bad thing? Why?

What changes to _____ would you recommend?

How effective are _____?

Do you agree with the actions of _____?

What is the importance of _____?

Would it be better if _____?

What would you select? Why?

Based on what you know, how would you explain_____?

Which method is most helpful? Why?

Category 3: How can we use this? Questions in this category require students to consider how particular information can be used. They require students to apply knowledge to a different context, make recommendations, transfer what they are learning to new problems or situations, and use the knowledge to solve a problem. The following question stems in this category are general examples that could be applied to any content area.

Application

Can you think of an example to fit this definition?"

What would happen if there were no _____?

What would happen if _____ were true?

Are the following statements fact or opinion? How did you determine that?

What if we changed _____?

Can you make a model to show that?

Can you write a similar problem?

How would this work with other problems?

How does this relate to _____?

Problem Solving

Suppose you were in _____ situation. How will this concept impact your actions?

How many ways can you come up with to _____?

Is there another way?

Suppose _____ were to happen. How would you solve it?

Based on what you know, how would you _____?

Writing good questions for your content. To adapt these generic question stems to specific content areas, consider the table below. I have selected a middle grades standard from different content areas and provided an example in each of the three categories.

Sample Standards	How do we make sense of this?
Language Arts Standard: Analyze how two or more authors writing about the same topic shape their presentations of key information by emphasizing the different evidence or advancing different interpretations of facts.	*Generic Stem:* What is the main point of the author's argument? How does he support it? *Content Question:* What is Lewis' main argument? How does he support it? What is Smith's main argument? How does she support it?
Math Standard: Apply properties of operations as strategies to add and subtract rational numbers.	*Generic Stem:* What is the rule? *Content Question:* Can you come up with a rule for adding integers?
Science Standard: Describe the structure and function of cells, tissues, organs, and organ systems.	*Generic Stem:* What is the relationship between ___and ___? *Content Question:* How is a living organism the sum of all its parts?
Social Studies Standard: Analyze cultural and ethnic diversity within the United States.	*Generic Stem:* What are ways that ____ have helped ___? *Content Question:* What are ways that different ethnic groups have contributed to the culture of the United States?

What do we think about this?	How do we use this?
Generic Stem: What does the author mean when he says _____? *Content Question:* What does Lewis mean when he says, "the room feels like space"? What does Smith mean when she says, "we are all lost"?	*Generic Stem:* Can you write a similar problem? *Content Question:* If you were to write an article on this issue, what would your argument be and how would you support it?
Generic Stem: What method is most helpful? Why? *Content Question:* What method for solving this problem is most helpful; why?"	*Generic Stem:* Suppose ____ were to happen. How would you solve it? *Content Question:* Suppose both negative numbers were fractions. How would you solve it?
Generic Stem: What is the importance of _____? *Content Question:* What is the importance of sunlight to plant and animal cells?	*Generic Stem:* Based on what you know, how would you ____? *Content Question:* Based on what you know, what do cells tell us about life and death?
Generic Stem: What is the value of _____? *Content Question:* What is the value of immigration?	*Generic Stem:* What would happen if ____ were true? *Content Question:* What would happen if no new immigrants were allowed into the country?

Probing. Asking probing questions leads your students to think deeply about a topic; your acquisition of this skill and teaching it to your students is a critical element of rich discussions. Socratic questioning, which is a disciplined method for focusing the exploration of an issue, is a good structure to assist you and your students. You might even create a wall poster for displaying these questions.

Socratic Questions

Clarifying questions
>What do you mean?
>Why do you say that?
>Could you explain that further?
>Can you elaborate on that?
>What exactly does this mean?
>Can you rephrase that?
>Are you saying _____ or _____?

Probing assumptions
>How can you verify or disprove that?
>Is that always the case?
>Why do you think that assumption holds true here?
>Please explain why/how_____.

Probing for reasons and evidence
>What would be an example?
>Why do you say that?
>Is there reason to doubt this evidence?
>Why is that happening?
>How do you know this?
>Are these reasons good enough?

Considering other viewpoints
>How would an opponent of this point of view respond?
>What is the counter argument for____?
>Did anyone see this another way?
>Does _____'s statement change anyone's mind?
>Another way to look at this is ____; does that seem reasonable?
>Why is it better than _____?

Probing implications and consequences
What are you implying?
But if ____ happened, what else would result?
How does ____ affect ____?
Then what would happen?
How could ____ be used to ____?

Question the question
Why do you think that I asked that question?
Why was that question important?
Which of your questions turned out to be the most useful?
Am I making sense? Why not?
What else might I ask?

Example of Using Probing Questions in a Discussion:

Teacher: What conclusions can we make about how the coefficient of x, or the slope, affects the line?

Students: (No one responds.)

Teacher: Viola, can you rephrase my question for me? I think the question might be a little tricky.

Viola: You want to know what happens to the line depending on what the number in front of x is. I think the bigger the number, the more slanted the line will be.

Teacher: Does anyone agree or disagree with Viola?

Nyema: I think she's right.

Teacher: How do you know?

Nyema: Well, when it was 4x + 2 it was more slanted than when it was 2x + 2.

Teacher: What do you think would happen if it was 2x + 6?

Beginning with a rich, high-level question and then using probing questions to move the discussion forward and challenge students to think deeply are critical steps for leading good class discussions. For more information about the Socratic Method and to see classroom examples, see Appendix D.

Chapter 3
Facilitating the Talk

Shifting your classroom emphasis from teacher talk to student talk may require a change in your role as teacher. As a facilitator, you focus more on your students' construction of understanding and less on delivering facts to be remembered by students (Cooke & Adams, 2003). You begin to transfer the responsibility for some of the control of the lesson direction to the students, which encourages them to take ownership of their learning and leads to their empowerment (Scott, 2003). This process of shifting ownership to students begins with valuing their ideas, helping them explore their ideas, and encouraging them to accept the ideas of others. This chapter provides practical strategies to help develop your skills as a facilitator who encourages productive student talk.

The most common form of classroom interaction is the Initiation-Response-Feedback (IRF) pattern (Mehan, 1979; Stigler & Hiebert, 1999). This interaction goes: the teacher asks a question (Initiation), the student responds (Response), and the teacher evaluates the response (Feedback).

Example of IRF interaction:
Teacher: What are the six kingdoms?
Francisco: Plantae, Animalia, Protista, Eubacteria, Archaebacteria, Fungi
Teacher: That's correct. You got all six!

While this common classroom interaction between one student and the teacher has some value, it comes to a resolution once the correct answer has been provided.

Funneling vs. Focusing

Wood (1998) discusses the concepts of Funneling and Focusing, which broaden the interactions that occur. Funneling occurs when the teacher asks a series of questions that lead the students to a pre-determined correct answer. For example:

Example of Funneling:
Teacher: What percent is ¾ equal to?
Students: (No response)
Teacher: Would it help if I changed it to a decimal first?
Ariel: I guess.
Teacher: How do I change a fraction to a decimal?
Ariel: Divide.
Teacher: Okay, Holly, if I divide 3 by 4 what do I get?
Holly (using calculator): .75
Teacher: That is correct. Now I have a decimal, how do I get it to a percent?
Jeremiah: Move the decimal two places.
Teacher: Which way?"
Jeremiah: To the right.
Teacher: So, who can tell me what percent ¾ is equal to?
Eduardo: 75%

While this interaction did involve more students and did seem more like a discussion, the class simply worked through the steps as the teacher directed and arrived at the correct answer. He funneled them in a pre-determined direction.

Wood (1998) suggests focusing as a more productive approach for engaging students to think critically and deeply. Focusing requires the teacher to listen to students' responses and guide them based on how they are thinking. So, the content objectives are covered, but the teacher does not determine ahead of time exactly how the class will arrive there. For example:

Example of Focusing:
Teacher: How did the author set the tone for the story?
Marcus: It was very serious and kind of sad.
Teacher: So, Marcus thinks the tone was serious and sad. Do others agree?
Students: (Nod their heads in agreement)
Teacher: What makes you think that it was serious and sad? What did the author do to create that tone?
Jasmine: Well, for one thing there wasn't any joking or laughter.
Xavier: And he said in this sentence that Jack was crying.
Teacher: So, it was partly what he included and partly what he didn't include?
Xavier: Yes, he left out things that are the opposite of sadness like laughing and he included things that tell you there is sadness, like crying.
Teacher: What are other methods of setting the tone for the story?
Felipe: Well it could also be by the characters' actions. If the characters are doing things like skipping in the park, it sets a happy tone, but if they are walking in a funeral procession, it sets a sad tone.
Teacher: Who can summarize the ways we discussed that an author can set the tone of a story?

In this excerpt, the teacher facilitated a discussion that led to covering her content objective, but she did not necessarily know the path ahead of time. However, she did ask questions that kept the class focused in the direction she wanted them to go.

Helpful phrases to focus (rather than funnel):

We're almost there. Can you find the last piece?
Can you develop that further?
Can you elaborate?
Okay, but is there more to it?
How did you come up with that?

Troubleshooting. Avoid prompting students to say the answer you are thinking or to follow the order of your reasoning, which quickly become games to guess what's in your head instead of processes to discover new knowledge and ideas. If students put their ideas up for examination and feedback from their peers, they have a chance to revise their beliefs based on evidence and install information in their long-term memory.

Take a Positive Approach

Good discussions can happen in an encouraging, positive classroom atmosphere. The classroom must be a safe place where risk taking is applauded and the teacher encourages and recognizes students' contributions. The teacher reinforces responses by eye contact, smiling, using a friendly tone, nodding the head, or in some way acknowledging a student's attempt to respond. Of course, the teacher must project enthusiasm about the topic—if the teacher is neither interested in nor engaged in the topic, students will not be.

Rick Wormeli (2013) writes about the importance of getting students to ask questions themselves so that they move information into their long-term memory during class discussions.

> Whoever asks the questions does the learning…As often as possible, ask students to brainstorm questions, queries, and investigate starting points for as many topics as time allows to get them in the habit….We're trying to make students so curious that they form their own questions: "Why does it do it?" "What will the effect be?" "What are the exceptions to this rule?" "Why do you believe that?" "How is this false?" "Where's my mistake?" and "what would happen if ____?"

> We can create curiosity by presenting students with puzzling phenomena, surprising facts, challenges to accepted opinions, appeals to imagination, playful situations with manipulatives connections among seemingly disparate concepts, moral dilemmas, and personal dramas when facing struggle. (224–225)

A "deficit approach," trying to catch unprepared students or students not paying attention by calling on them, does not build a positive climate that encourages students to participate. In fact, it has the opposite effect: Students will avoid talking because they do not want to be caught unprepared. Trying to catch students when you think they may have something to contribute lends itself to a healthier, more robust discussion. A strategy for the student who is unprepared or not paying attention is to discreetly give the student a warning that you will be calling on him/her in 2 minutes to contribute.

Helpful phrases for getting peers to build on reluctant students' contributions:

Jess, you're in the neighborhood. Can anyone add to Jess's idea?
I like your reasoning. Malia, can you add any evidence for that argument?
You are working hard to contribute today. Julio, did you use the same process?
That's a good beginning, take it from there, Kevin.

Troubleshooting:

1. Avoid letting incorrect information stand. Be positive, but evaluate every contribution. You do not want to create a scenario in which everyone contributes random ideas and all ideas are accepted without evaluation You can reinforce someone's effort while at the same time correcting a content error he or she introduced to the discussion. Rick Wormeli (2013) offers these strategies for correcting false information without having the students shut down by the teacher's negating of their comments:

   • Act interested in understanding the students' comments, even when you're not...ask students to tell you more about their statement or idea. By explaining their point further, they eventually discover the fallacy of their thinking, which is much more effective than when we point out the fallacies to them.

- Share empathy. Tell students that you used to think this way (even if you didn't) but that you changed your mind once you read and considered the information at the bottom of page (insert whatever was the page intended for last night's reading, which this student failed to do). You might frame it as, "I understand how you could conclude...but let's see if the text information changes your thinking."

- Alter the current reality. When a student responds to a question with an incorrect answer, change your question to be one for which the student's response is the correct answer. Go on from there and re-ask the intended question of someone else. You can also re-ask the question of the earlier student after a period of clarifying conversation with the class.

- Do not accept "I don't know" as an answer. Turn it around quickly and say, "If you did know, what would you have said?" ...Very often, they answer fully, and what they say is actually on target. They just didn't trust themselves. This strategy is safe for the hesitant student because it is just a conjecture that will be considered but not judged.

- Allow the student more time or to ask for assistance: "Would you like to text a friend...or ask for assistance from somebody in the room?"

- Affirm the portions that are correct and disregard the other elements. (pp. 225–226)

2. Avoid personal criticism and sarcasm which create a hostile environment full of fear. They are neither respectful nor effective in engaging students. Compare the results of the following interactions:

Example of an unproductive class discussion:
Teacher: Do you see a relationship between the 3 sides?
Jess: They make a triangle.
Teacher (sighing): That's obvious Jess—a 7-year-old could have told me that. Does anyone see a relationship between the measurements of the 3 sides? Jose?
Jose: (Shrugs and says nothing)
Teacher: Jose, you need to start paying attention. Does anyone else have an idea?
Class: (No one responds.)

Example of a productive class discussion:
Teacher: Do you see a relationship between the 3 sides?
Jess: They make a triangle.
Teacher: That is one observation, Jess. Does anyone see a relationship between the measurements of the 3 sides? Jose?
Jose: (Shrugs and says nothing)
Teacher: I know you can do this, Jose. Why don't you play around with those 3 numbers on your calculator for a minute, and I'll come back to you.
Teacher: What ideas do other people have?
Shanika: All of the numbers are odd.
Teacher: That's an interesting observation. We'll add that to the list and see if it is significant as we go. So far, we know that it is a triangle and all of the measurements are odd. What else can we observe?

Everyone Contributes

This is easier said than done. It is important to set the expectation for everyone to participate in classroom discussions, both small group discussions and whole class discussions. At the beginning of the year, emphasize that everyone contributing during discussions is critical because they will all learn the material better if they are always engaged and preparing to offer input into discussions, and learning to contribute now will help them in the future. Explain how you and their classmates will support them to succeed by making it comfortable for them to talk in front of others and by respecting their ideas.

Also, help them realize that they are not alone if they feel some fear of speaking in groups—many middle school students are with new classmates and are learning new communication skills at the same time. Show that you value everyone's contributions by using positive body language and really listening to their contributions. Create an atmosphere where it is not stressful for students to participate by offering supportive comments, using an encouraging tone of voice, smiling, and demonstrating through body language and facial expressions that you are interested in their thoughts.

Impact of social class. In *Teaching with Poverty in Mind*, Erick Jensen (2009) says that although

> ...children in poverty are more likely to describe feeling deprived, embarrassed, picked on, and bullied....feel[ing] isolated and unworthy in their younger years,...the [common] assumption that they won't succeed at school because of their home lives is not supported by research. Teachers are in an opportune position to provide strong relationship support. (p. 87)

Students from low income families are more likely to have less secure attachments and stable environments than other students and may require more support in learning to build positive relationships both with their peers and teachers. Learning to positively bond with peers and teachers can improve their self-esteem and academic progress. Jensen goes on to advise:

What you want to emphasize at school is moderate social status and group acceptance. The best thing you or your staff can do is include, include, include. Help students feel accepted for who they are, and give them all micro-niches for status by finding some tasks or narrow skill or knowledge sets at which they excel.... When students feel accepted, have sufficient social status, and maintain positive relationships, they bloom academically. (p. 90)

Wait time. The research on wait time tells us to wait three to seven seconds for a response. Stepping in too quickly to help or ask others to help a student sends the message, "I know you can't do this" to not only the student but also the rest of the class. In her book *Fall Down 7 Times Get Up 8: Teaching Kids to Succeed* (2012), Debbie Silver tells of her worry about traumatizing a student if she didn't "rescue" him and describes what might have been a stronger outcome after the seven seconds had elapsed.

At that point, rather than moving away from the student, I needed to provide cues, prompts, and further questions to help clarify the answer. Like most teachers, I made my decisions based on best intentions. I didn't want the student to be embarrassed. I thought I was rescuing him. But now, I'm embarrassed by all those missed opportunities to help my reluctant participants gain a little autonomy. (p. 123)

Start with a reluctant talker first. I learned one technique for engaging reluctant students from a graduate school professor who was the master of giving everyone a place to enter the conversation. She would call on her lower-level students or on a more reluctant student first. She let them begin the conversation with rudimentary ideas and then asked others to build on those thoughts. Although the class was over my head, I learned from this brilliant teacher that it is easier to enter a discussion at the beginning rather than at the middle or the end.

Coaching the reluctant talker. For students paralyzed with fear at the thought of talking during class discussion or those whose writings show depth of thought on the topics of class but who naturally hold back from contributing, individual coaching may provide support not only of their ability to participate in class discussions, but also in their gaining self-efficacy and lifelong skills that will greatly impact their lives. Find out why they don't contribute and then discuss whatever issues are holding them back. Many middle school students feel that everyone is judging them all the time; help them see the reality of everyone being in the same boat. If everyone in class stopped talking, it would be a dull class and opportunity to learn from each other would be stifled.

Check to see whether the students feel they do not have the ability to participate in a productive way—what Debbie Silver (2012) calls a fixed mindset. If they only feel smart when they don't make mistakes, work fast, or the work is easy for them but hard for others—it's about being perfect right now for them. Challenge them to move to a growth mindset: when it's really hard, they try really hard and learn to do something they couldn't do before; they can figure something out over a long period of time and be successful.

Mistakes are opportunities. Create an environment where mistakes are seen as learning opportunities and are not devastating to a student's self-esteem. Explicitly state that learning can occur from incorrect or incomplete answers and give examples of great inventors whose success was begun from mistakes. Allow students to make false starts.

We're in it together. Encourage students to help each other when someone gets stuck while making a contribution. Establish the idea that finding a solution to the question is the responsibility of the whole class. McCann, Johannessen,

Kahn, and Flanagan (2006) suggest a scaffolding strategy for particularly reluctant students: Ask the question. Wait time. Rephrase the question. Offer some choices. Or, offer what a person might think a reasonable answer is and ask the student if s/he agrees or disagrees and why.

Move around. Another important strategy is to move away from the front of the room. Sit on the side of the room or in the back. Sit down, rather than stand. Or if you choose to stand, then move around and do not stand in one place. This helps to develop the idea that students are talking to each other, rather than the traditional teacher–student–teacher–student pattern.

Random generator. Finally, we have a tendency to call on the same small group of students who are eager to participate and tend to give us correct answers. To avoid this trap, try utilizing a random generator strategy of which there are several. One of the tried-and-true favorites is popsicle sticks with student names written on them. Or a stack of cards, each having a student's name. There is also a random name picker on classtools.net or you can use a mobile app such as "List Selector" that will randomly select a name from a list you enter. Utilizing one of these techniques helps ensure that everyone is a part of the discussion, not just a select few. I recommend that whatever method you use, put the student's name back into the "pile" after you call on them. This eliminates the expectation that once called upon, students can check out mentally from the discussion.

Helpful phrases:

We will help you.
Just give us an idea to get us started thinking.
_____, are you thinking?
_____, I'll let you think for a second and then I'll come back to you for an idea.

Troubleshooting:

1. Everyone doesn't have to participate in every whole class discussion in order to set the expectation that everyone contributes. Thirty students times 1 minute-per-contribution is too long for most discussions—at this length they would drag, losing everyone's attention. Although everyone doesn't have to speak in every discussion, everyone does have to speak in some discussions. It is not okay for a group of students never to speak, no matter how shy they are.

2. Do not fall into the trap of answering your own questions. Sometimes there will be silence, and you have to be okay with that. If students can answer every question quickly without any hesitation, then your questions are too low-level. If you expect students to answer challenging questions, they will need some time to think. Use the strategy of wait time; if you fill the void of silence with your answer, students will quickly learn that they can sit back and let you do the heavy lifting.

Example of expecting everyone to contribute:

Teacher: Ryan what techniques did the author use to build suspense in the story?

Ryan: I don't know.

Teacher: Think back to when you were reading the story. When did you start wondering what was going to happen next?

Ryan: I don't know.

Teacher: Okay, I'll give you a minute to go back and skim the story so you can find an example. I'll come back to you.

Start Small and Go Big

This strategy is a direct result of personal experience. I am a reflective thinker (and so are many students). When I was in graduate school, class discussions were common. As the discussion progressed, someone would make a comment triggering a thought that I would debate in my mind for a few moments to determine whether or not I believed it was worthy to be shared with the group. If I decided it was, then I would spend a bit of time framing my statement and determining how I wanted to share the idea. By this time, the discussion had moved in a different direction, and my idea was now off point. Although I had been paying attention and was mentally engaged in the discussion, as a reflective thinker, it took me longer to frame my thoughts in a way that they could be shared, and I missed my window of opportunity.

The solution for getting reflective thinkers into discussion is to start with a small audience (of the individual herself or a small group) and go big (to the whole class). Pose the question and give students time to write down their thoughts individually. Or pose the question and give them an opportunity to discuss the question in small groups before having the whole class discussion. All of the whole class discussion structures in Chapter 5 provide this opportunity for students to put their thoughts together about a topic before having to engage in the discussion.

Starting small and going big has many benefits. It gives students time to explore the content information they need in order to successfully discuss the question. It helps to focus students' attention and to stimulate their thoughts initially. Sharing attitudes, thoughts, and opinions in small groups first allows for more student involvement and gives students more time to capitalize on a student's basic desire to talk (Theobald, 2003). It also requires impulsive students who are comfortable thinking out loud to organize their thoughts and determine which are the most important before sharing them with the class. Contributions will be stronger if students have time to prepare and the discussion will, therefore, be more interesting.

Troubleshooting: Stopping after the small group discussion gives you no way of knowing the quality of each group's discussion. Even if you actively monitor the groups, you cannot hear everything said in each group. Some groups could form misconceptions; other groups could miss identifying key concepts; a group could have been totally off topic. The "starting small" part needs to be followed by the "going big" part every time. You must ensure that everyone gets to hear the correct information to understand the lesson objectives.

Stay on Topic

Theobald (2003) found that students actually disliked off-task discussions. We have likely all gotten frustrated when a topic is under discussion and an idea from left field suddenly takes the conversation in an unhelpful direction. While encouraging students to take ownership of their learning and to become more independent, you are still responsible as the facilitator to keep the discussion focused on the planned topic. Here are several strategies.

Project the question. Throughout the discussion, project the topic or question to the front of the room. In addition to the benefit of pairing of auditory and visual directions, this also allows you to refocus the discussion by pointing to the question if the class gets off-track—you can have everyone look at the board and reread the question if necessary.

Note-taking on board. Have someone take notes on the board for everyone to see. If you have a computer connected to a projector, someone can just type ideas as they are shared underneath the question, or they could write notes on the white board. If you have the luxury of a co-teacher, this is an ideal job for him or her, or perhaps you can let students take turns being the scribe. If all else fails, you can put notes on the board as new ideas are shared. Indicate important points by underlining them or putting a star beside them. Another benefit of this strategy is that it prevents students from continually repeating an idea that has already been shared. If you put asides and important ideas to be considered later in a separate but visible place, students can "let go" of ideas that are important to them but not related to the topic.

Intervene verbally. You can stop the discussion at some point and provide a summary or ask students to draw conclusions about what has been discussed so far. Another intervention is to ask students to briefly discuss with a partner the last point shared. Or, you can simply redirect the students back to the question they should be discussing.

Helpful phrases:

The question we are thinking about right now is_____.

Help me see how _____ relates to _____.

Let's look again at the question on the board. Let's return to that question.

We're discussing _____. Who has a thought about that?

Troubleshooting:

1. Don't take the discussion off-track yourself—my own most common mistake in facilitating a discussion. Once a student comment triggers a memory of a funny story, I just "have to" share it and get a laugh. Again, the teacher must model the behavior s/he wants his/her students to emulate.

2. Staying on topic does not mean that the students have to follow your plan exactly as you designed it. When you really listen to your students, you may hear them making a connection to another topic (even another subject area) that may be worth exploring. Although you work very hard to make your lessons relevant, supporting students

in making connections is an even higher priority because it "cements" their learning. I once observed a teacher lecturing on Nelson Mandela, and a student said something about him being like Ghandi. Ignoring the comment, she continued with her PowerPoint, missing an opportunity for students to take the discussion down a meaningful path and take ownership in their learning. It is a balancing act to remain in charge of the class while supporting students making critical, relevant connections to their present knowledge and world—even if you did not pre-plan them.

Example of Bringing a Discussion Back on Topic:

Teacher: Why do you think the Soviet Union would not allow Eastern European countries to participate in the Marshall Plan?

Emiyo: Probably just because they wanted power and didn't want to share it with other countries.

Daniela: Yeah, kind of like when teachers are power hungry and they won't let students do anything.

Terrance: Tell me about it. They won't even let us go to our lockers between classes anymore.

Teacher: I see your concern about not having personal power. Let's think about the Soviet Union. What would be the problem with allowing the Eastern European countries to be a part of the Marshall Plan?

Require Evidence

Middle school students definitely have a lot of opinions—just ask them; they will be happy to share them with you! During the middle grades, early adolescents begin to think abstractly and to consider points of view other than their own. The Common Core State Standards (CCSS) require that we hold students responsible for backing up their ideas and stances with specific evidence or details from texts. "The implication for instruction is that we ask students to study the text and cite specific words of the author to back up their ideas or make well-founded inferences that they can clearly substantiate" (Spencer, 2013). Just saying, "I think ____ is true, just because I believe it," should not cut it in your classroom.

One strategy is to ask students to read the part of the text that backs up their statement to the class. Another strategy is to offer a counterexample that contradicts their statement and ask them to verify which is correct by citing evidence. You may even want to stop a discussion at some point and ask the class to work with a partner to create a list of three pieces of evidence that verifies the last point a person made in the discussion. An important life skill for students to develop is their ability to convince others that their ideas are valid.

Helpful Phrases:

How do you know that?
Is there anything in the chapter that backs up what you said?
If the governor (or other appropriate official) were to walk in right now and disagree with you, how could you show him or her that you are correct?
How can you justify that?
How can we verify whether or not that is true?
What if someone said you were wrong about that? How would you respond?
It seems like you're giving this some thought. Tell me two things that are coming to mind.

Troubleshooting:

1. Avoid requiring evidence for every contribution because this bogs down the discussion and quickly becomes tedious. To be sure, it is critical that students regularly provide evidence for their statements with the ultimate goal of their doing this by habit and without being asked.

2. Avoid jumping in too quickly and telling students they are wrong. Try to create an atmosphere in which student ideas and thoughts, whether supportive or contradictory, are welcomed and respectfully delivered. Teach the students to respond to each other, and let them be the first to address a student who may have said something of questionable accuracy. Setting up a scenario of two students defending opposite positions with the rest of the class verifying the more valid position based on evidence is a golden teaching moment. At times, you will have to correct content errors because they can't just linger in the air, but if you can facilitate students helping each other to find meaning based on evidence, that is the ideal.

Example of Requiring Evidence:

Brian: Our group said that Americans didn't trust Japanese people.

Teacher: That's a big statement to say that a whole country didn't trust a whole other country. What evidence do you have?

Jada: Well, the United States was on the side of the Allied powers and Japan was on the side of the Axis powers.

Brian: And the United States took China's side against Japan.

Teacher: How did they do that?

Shanice: Well, they blocked trade with Japan and they sent supplies and troops to China.

Teacher: What other evidence do we have that there was distrust between Americans and Japanese? I'm not convinced.

Raisa: Well the Japanese bombed us at Pearl Harbor. That's enough to make me not trust you.

Teacher: That's a good point Raisa, but it helps to convince me that the two countries were enemies. Is it fair to say that all Americans didn't trust all Japanese people because the two countries were on opposite sides of the war?

Jada: Well what about the internment camps? Japanese people were being locked up by the U.S. government. If I'm just a regular citizen of California and I see the government locking up a whole race of people, it would make me question things.

Raisa: So maybe we should say the two countries were enemies and didn't trust each other, and most Americans didn't trust Japanese people. My dad constantly tells me that you should never say always or never, because there is always an exception. I bet we could find some guy that was an American living in Oregon who was friends with his Japanese neighbor across the street.

Teacher: I agree with that conclusion Raisa. You all have convinced me that the U.S. and Japan were on opposite sides during the war and gave a lot of evidence that there was general distrust between the two countries and their citizens but not necessarily every American distrusted every Japanese person.

Make it Relevant

One of the 16 key characteristics of middle level education according to the Association for Middle Level Education is, "The curriculum is challenging, exploratory, integrative, and relevant" (NMSA, 2010, p.14). I want to focus on the last word, relevant. Seeing how what they are learning is relevant to their lives, students will more actively engage in your class discussions. Making connections to other subjects and current events are ways to pique students' interest.

Helpful Phrases:
Does this remind anyone of something in their lifetime?
Do you know anyone like this?
What is this like?
How would that work today?

Troubleshootiing:
1. Avoid detours down long, winding roads as you focus on relevancy and connections. Maintain the focus and majority of the time on the content at hand. Sometimes a brief mention of something from their lives is all you need to get them thinking.

2. Also, you have to work at being "current"—what was cool and hip when you were in middle school isn't anymore. Take the time to listen to your students and watch some of their television shows to know their interests; this tells them that you care about them and helps them trust you.

Example of Students Making Connections:

Teacher: What were the results of the bombings of Hiroshima and Nagasaki?

Brian: Well for starters over 100,000 people were killed.

Adrienne: How many were killed in the Boston Marathon bombing?

Teacher: That's a good connection Adrienne. Three people lost their lives in that bombing on Monday. Think about how much that has affected our country this week. Can you imagine if 100,000 people had been killed?

Antonio: Yeah, and it didn't happen in just one part of the city, it was the WHOLE city. Well TWO WHOLE cities.

Maintain Neutrality

In our efforts to encourage student participation, we offer a constant stream of positive reinforcement. These good intentions create a couple of unintended problems. Students begin to look for validation for their contributions, and the teacher remains in the position of expert. What happens if you don't immediately agree and thereby offer your stamp of approval? Ask other students what they think. The goal is to have students become the experts and to determine whether or not they are accurate in their thinking without relying solely on the teacher. If students don't have the evidence to cite, you can refer them to the text or other resources as they determine the validity of an answer.

In addition, there is not always a simple right or wrong answer to the many complex issues in life. You must teach your students to accept differences of opinion and to learn the skills for understanding all sides of an issue. Sometimes it is through the discussion of unresolved issues that students learn to ultimately accept differences in one another. It is during the early adolescent years that students are able to begin accepting some ambiguity and to consider alternative viewpoints. When maintaining neutrality during heated discussions, try to avoid comments supporting one side, such as *right, very good,* or *exactly.*

Helpful Phrases to use:

I hadn't thought of that.
That raises another interesting point.
That really forces us to think of the issue in another way.

Example of Maintaining Neutrality:

Trevon: I think Jack made the story more interesting. If he hadn't been in this book, I would have never finished it. It was boring.

Teacher: You think so?

Aran: I didn't like Jack. I thought he was rude and always had to have his way. Basically, I thought he was a jerk.

Teacher: I wonder, Aran, do you think Trevon was saying that he liked Jack or that he thought Jack made the book more interesting. Those sound like two different things to me.

Trevon: I wasn't saying I want to make the guy my best friend; I was just saying that the story would have been boring without him in it.

Teacher: Class, what do we call that kind of character? The kind of character that seems to always be causing problems?

Disagree Agreeably

Knowing how to disagree respectfully is an important discussion skill. The Common Core collaborative standards expect students to "follow rules for collegial discussions." In our current global, collaborative community, an important workplace skill is the ability to work productively to find common ground with those with whom you disagree. One need only look at the statistics of the number of fights in middle schools last year to realize that this is a helpful life skill that many early adolescents lack. The School Survey on Crime and Safety (National Center for Educational Statistics, 2011) reports that middle schools have higher rates of violent incidents (40.0 per 1000 students) than elementary (21.3 per 1000 students) and high school (21.4 per 1000 students).

Ask a clarifying question. Often arguments begin as simple misunderstandings and miscommunications. People of all ages tend to make assumptions about what another person really means or what motive is behind his statement. One strategy for improving communication is to teach students to ask a clarifying question when someone says something they disagree with. Clarifying question stems are:

- When you said_____, what did you mean?
- I'm not sure I understood what you meant by _____.
- Could you explain that again?
- Can you say that another way?

Rationale for disagreement. Require students to give a rationale for their disagreements. Take some time at the beginning of the year to demonstrate ways to politely disagree with someone.

As the year goes on, if a student forgets to do this, then stop the student and model how to state an opinion. Require the student to restate his or her objection politely.

Polite disagreement phrases. Teach students helpful phrases to say they disagree in a polite way, such as those that follow. You also have to establish that put-downs are not allowed.

- I understand your point, but I have another opinion.

- I am not sure I completely agree with that. What about…...

- I would like to challenge her on that.

- I'm not sure I'm completely sold on that. What about_____?

Example of disagreeing agreeably:
Teacher: Let's talk about the venn diagrams that you all made in your groups. What are some differences in the inner and outer planets?
Chin: Even though the outer planets are bigger, the inner planets are heavier.
Teacher: Sarah, how did your group come to that conclusion?
Sarah: Well the thing on the computer said that the outer planets were gaseous and the inner planets are solid. Gas is lighter than a solid.
Enrique: And it also said that the inner planets were made up of heavy metals like iron and nickel, and they are more dense.
Jamal: Well, I disagree with the fact that if they are more dense they are heavier. The outer planets are bigger. A golf ball is denser than a basketball, but a basketball is heavier. And it's full of air.
Teacher: Okay, Jamal is bringing up a counter example to back up his disagreement. That is a good technique. So let's try to resolve this disagreement by looking back at the definitions of density and weight. I think it's important to make sure we understand those terms and how they apply here. Who can tell me what density means?

The class goes on to define weight and density, and the teacher points out that since they are two different concepts, you can't automatically conclude that since something is denser, it is necessarily heavier or vice versa. Enrique makes a joke about weighing a planet on a scale. The teacher sends Enrique and Jamal to the computer to see if they can find any information about which planets are the heaviest. The teacher then continues on with the original question by calling on another group to share something from their venn diagram.

Manage Hot Topics During Discussions

In the course of discussing issues of relevance to them, middle school students will encounter opportunities to learn from their classmates' differing opinions and values. The teacher's responsibility is to help students learn from the moment while protecting all parties involved. In "Managing Hot Moments in the Classroom," Lee Warren says that making difficult, uncomfortable events (hot moments) productive requires "getting out of our own emotional confusion [and] beginning to see the heat as an opportunity to explore different views about the topic" (2002-2006). He counsels teachers to keep the environment stable for students by remaining steady, breathing deeply, and taking a moment of silence. Further, to avoid taking remarks personally, he suggests teachers become aware of what issues are most likely to push their buttons and have strategies already in place for managing the class when hot topics are under discussion. Warren goes on to suggest helping students think about hot topics by:

- Not permitting personal attacks and being open to multiple perspectives which students argue responsibly.

- Taking the issue off individuals making offensive remarks and putting it on the table for general discussion.

- Requiring all students to understand each other's perspectives—"Ask them to listen carefully to the other point of view, ask questions, and then restate or argue that position."

- Asking students to write reflectively and then discuss the issue or to research outside of class and write a balanced essay.

- Talking with students outside of class. Help them learn about themselves and others, the topic, and how to voice their positions so that they will be heard even by those who disagree.

- Giving an extremely distressed student a chance to leave the classroom to calm down after acknowledging the outburst (2002–2006).

Failure to address students' hurtful remarks about gender, race, politics, and religion teaches them their behavior is acceptable and teaches other students that they are not protected. It negates the opportunity for students to explore a wide range of ideas.

Listening

Listening is an important skill involved in talking with others. The two go hand-in-hand, although many of us forget that on a day-to-day basis. Being quiet while someone else is talking is not really listening. The key to real listening is sincerely wanting to learn from someone else. As the teacher, you must consciously listen. Teachers are used to doing the talking, and most of us are not as practiced at listening. But it is also important to explicitly teach your students to listen. Take some class time to share these tips.

First, show that you are listening. Maintain good eye contact, nod your head occasionally, and lean slightly forward. Our facial expressions and body language speak volumes about whether we are really listening or not.

Second, practice active listening. Ask the speaker questions to clarify his or her meaning; paraphrase what the speaker is saying; relate the speaker's statement to your own perspective.

Helpful phrases:
What I hear you saying is____.
Do you mean____?
Listening to what you said, I wonder if____.

Troubleshooting:
1 Avoid interrupting. People tend to interrupt when they aren't really listening. While the other person is speaking, their mind focuses on what they are going to say next. They just "buy time" to prepare their next comment and get tired of waiting.

2. Avoid listening only for the weak points in a student's argument so that you can prove her wrong. Listen to all the student says so that you can better understand the context and the intent of her statements.

Developing Facilitation Skills

Facilitating healthy discussions is actually an advanced skill for teachers. It is the rare beginning teacher who can successfully balance all of the things discussed in this book. You need to practice and continually endeavor to improve the quality of the discussions in your classroom. Here are some practical ideas for doing that.

First, videotape a class discussion. When you view the tape, pay attention to who is doing the talking and to the quality of the contributions. Notice how deep the conversation went or whether it stayed superficial. Were your learning objectives achieved? By whom? I have learned a tremendous amount from watching videos of my teaching. Sometimes what I felt in the moment was an amazing lesson turned out to be only two students talking with me while the rest of the class quietly tuned out.

Second, watch other teachers. When you are sitting in the back of the room without the pressure of keeping an entire room of middle grades students engaged, you can easily gain insight into what works and what doesn't. Also, pay attention to how group discussions work in church, civic organizations, or social gatherings. Note when people are talking "at" each other, rather than "with" each other.

Third, invite a good friend to observe your class. Ask a colleague for honest feedback about whatever he notices, or ask him to look for specific aspects related to your goals. For example, if you have noticed a weakness in students asking questions of each other and have set strengthening that as an objective, your observer could record the number of students asking questions of each other and whether or not you seized opportunities to support students' development in this area. Using that as a baseline, your friend could repeat this observation later and a comparison of the data would serve as formative assessment.

Chapter 4
Establishing and Maintaining a Respectful Community

There are some students who, we suspect, came out of the womb talking. Having outgoing personalities, they love to talk in groups and participate regularly in class. Comfortable thinking out loud, they don't need confidence that their thoughts are well-developed before speaking in front of a group. Sometimes their contributions are on target and sometimes, not.

In my experience, these students are the minority. Most early adolescents are reticent about sharing their academic ideas in class for a variety of reasons that include low self-esteem and fear of ridicule, whether it is subtle or blatant. Peer approval is a high priority for early adolescents. Another reason for not sharing could be lack of preparation from neglecting the background reading or note-taking.

It is the teacher's responsibility to establish an environment that supports student talk in the classroom. With actions and with words, a teacher can say, "I know this is difficult, but I believe you can do it and I believe it is important for you to succeed at collaborating with other people." Furthermore, it is the teacher's responsibility to ensure that every student succeed in this area. This chapter will discuss what teachers should do to prepare themselves and their students for class discussions and will share practical strategies for managing the issues that can prevent effective classroom talk such as noise level, off-task behaviors, and argumentative positions otherwise known as typical middle school behaviors.

Rules for Collegial Discussions

Establishing a classroom community and an atmosphere of respect for others is a critical part of productive class discussions. This work begins at the beginning of the year and must be diligently worked on throughout the year. You cannot let up.

When you are establishing the classroom procedures at the beginning of the year, you should also establish rules for discussions (Palmer, 2011). Talk with students about the importance of dialogue in learning and why you will be using it as a learning strategy for them. Let them know having productive discussions in which everyone participates requires a safe environment where everyone feels comfortable talking about social studies (or science, or math, etc.). Early adolescents seek approval from their peers and are not going to take risks in front of peers during academic discussions if they believe they might be ridiculed. Some students are shy and speaking in groups is especially difficult for them. As the teacher, you are responsible for establishing an environment where discomfort for speaking in groups is minimized.

Set clear expectations before the first class discussion. Here are some classroom rules that you might select from:
1. It is important not to laugh at the ideas of others.
2. One person speaks at a time.
3. Listen patiently. Do not interrupt someone else.

4. Respect all opinions and contributions and disagree agreeably.

5. Be kind and tolerant.

6. Build on others' ideas in a polite way.

7. Stay on topic.

8. Have calm discussions in quiet voices.

Student ownership of the rules. You might want to give students ownership in the rules—you could ask them to brainstorm what they think are the most important things they value in an environment safe to discuss issues. Compile their ideas (adding to the list anything you deem essential that they missed), post the rules, and then hold them accountable for adhering to them.

Applying the rules. Set up a discussion about a non-academic topic of interest to the class. Give students cards with lines to read. Assign a student to behave inappropriately and then have the class talk about how he should have behaved. Or you could play the role of the inappropriate speaker. For example, a student could state her opinion and you interrupt them, rolling your eyes, laughing, etc. Let the students tell you what you did wrong and what you should have done. Or, show short video clips of people having discussions with inappropriate behavior (television is rampant with examples) and then show examples of people having discussions appropriately (Palmer, 2011).

Modeling the rules. Probably the most important way that you can teach students to communicate respectfully is to model the behavior you wish them to emulate. If you want your students to listen patiently without interrupting each other, then you should listen patiently to them when they are speaking to you. If you want students to consider alternative viewpoints, then you should consider their points of view. Without losing control of the class, you can share your adult perspective as you speak kindly, politely, and respectfully to your students. This may sound easy, but watch as adults have conversations and notice how often this practice occurs.

Display posters. Another strategy for establishing a classroom community conducive to healthy discussions is to make posters for your classroom. Create posters that say things such as:

- Pursue Your Hunch.
- Justify
- Listen Patiently
- Back it Up with Evidence
- Analyze and Defend
- Respect Everyone's Opinion
- Be Kind and Tolerant
- Disagree Agreeably

Set expectations at the beginning of a discussion. When you are beginning a discussion, you may want to review the class expectations about acting and speaking respectfully and then be explicit about what you want from students in the particular discussion. If the class is brainstorming, then let them know any idea is welcomed. Or, if they are to cite evidence from text, tell them that ahead of time. If you are looking for as many ideas as possible, no matter the source, say so. If you want every person in the group to be able to explain the math problem, tell them that upfront.

Management Strategies

Once you have made your expectations explicit, you might find some or all of the following strategies helpful in maintaining that healthy classroom community.

Start with Partners

At the beginning of the year, it is not a good idea to jump right into groups of four and expect them to engage in a thought-provoking discussion about a high-level question for 30 minutes. You are setting your students up for failure. Start small. Begin with groups of two students working on one question that is a relatively low-hanging fruit. Select a question that is open-ended, yet not too difficult, and within the reach of everyone in the room. Over the first couple weeks of school, gradually increase the difficulty of the questions and the length of time the partners are asked to discuss them. To prevent chaos when transitioning from individual work to partner discussions, assign the students to work with their elbow partners. If they have a designated partner every time they are to share, it prevents confusion and off-task time.

Once your students have a good handle on discussing questions with partners, then you can gradually move to groups of three. Once that is going well, move to groups of four. Do not feel pressure to increase the group size too quickly—you want to be sure your students are successful and that you maintain control.

Word on the Board

This is hands-down the most effective management strategy I have ever used and the best idea that I have gotten from another teacher. I learned this from Teresa Harrell, one of the best 8th grade teachers I've ever worked with. Select a word. It could be your school mascot, the subject you teach, an important vocabulary term, or perhaps your last name.

The strategy is simple and works like this. When the noise level of the class is too high, or when you need the class's attention, you begin spelling the word on the board. When students notice you writing the word, that is their cue to get quiet, and they quietly signal others to do the same. As soon as the class is quiet, you stop writing. Give your instructions and allow the students to continue their discussion in a lower tone of voice, begin the whole class discussion, or do whatever you intended that needed their attention. If the noise level gets too high again, you begin writing where you left off the last time. If the class gets through the end of the period before the word is completely spelled, then everything is fine. However, if the word is finished before the class period, then everyone moves back to their individual desks, and they do boring worksheets for the rest of that class period and the entire next day.

Believe me, you will not have to spell the whole word more than once for any given class, and there will be some classes that never get to the last letter. They are tired of worksheets. They have seen enough of them. They like to talk and will do so within the parameters you set if you give them clear lines. The beauty of this strategy is that it gives the students wiggle room to be early adolescents. Early adolescents are not going to perform perfectly—that's not possible. Having the cue word allows them to get excited and talk a little louder than they should without suffering a consequence. But it does not allow them to continue talking louder than they should. It gives them boundaries, and allows for flexibility at the same time.

Too Noisy App

This is a mobile app that helps you monitor the noise level in the room. Once the teacher sets the sensitivity, the noise meter measures the volume of noise in the classroom. Once the noise level reaches too high it sounds an alarm. The app has a visual meter that can be displayed on the board to help students maintain an appropriate volume. The free app, Too Noisy, can be found at http://toonoisyapp.com/

The acceptable level of class noise depends on what the class is doing at any particular time, so the teacher can adjust the sensitivity of the meter accordingly. Students can see whether they are too loud and can encourage each other to quiet down, which saves the teacher countless times of drawing students' attention to the noise level and maintains student focus on the work.

10–15 Minute Rule

In general, you can expect early adolescents to stay engaged in an activity for about 10–15 minutes at the most—including class discussions. Any activity that lasts longer than that has a tendency to lead to distracted students and off-task behavior. Some questions may only need to be talked about for a few minutes, but even discussions about the best, in-depth questions should not last longer than 10–15 minutes. One option to consider is to allow the small group discussion to last about 5–10 minutes and then switch to a whole class discussion that lasts no longer than 10 minutes.

Alternative Assignment

This is the ultimate consequence for an off-task student, or an off-task group. Early adolescents are peer-oriented, so use this as leverage in your favor. If you notice a student or a group engaged in off-task behavior or conversing about the wrong topic, simply walk over and give them a calm warning. Remind them of the question they should be discussing and let them know they will only be allowed to work together on the question if they are on-topic. If the off-task behavior continues or happens again, then separate the students. Each student has to continue answering the question in writing individually, rather than being allowed to collaborate with others. If applied consistently, this will quickly eliminate off-topic conversations. Early adolescents will do what they have to in order to be able to talk with peers.

Have a Signal

If you have students discussing a question in small groups, you need a method to get their attention and bring them back together for the whole class discussion. Yelling "Let me have your attention" or "Listen up" are not effective. As the year progresses, your yelling will get louder and louder. It is much more effective to have an agreed-upon signal that students know means for them to get quiet and give you their attention. Find a signal that you are comfortable using. Here are some examples.

Rainstick—Said to have originated with the Aztec, a rainstick is a musical instrument that makes a sound like rain falling when it is turned upside down. It's a calming method for getting your students' attention.

If you can hear me clap once—The teacher says in a normal tone of voice: "If you can hear me, clap once." Students who hear it respond by clapping once. Then the teacher says in a quieter voice: "If you can hear me, clap twice." Everyone claps twice. By this time the room will be quiet enough for the students to hear you give instructions.

Clapping Rhythm—This is a commonly used method. The teacher claps a rhythm of about 5 claps, and the students respond with the same clap. The students know this is their signal to be quiet and look at the teacher.

Bear Chant—I saw a teacher use this on the 6th grade Bears team. They had a team chant that went something like this:
>Teacher: What do bears do?
>Students (in unison): Climb high!

From small groups to whole class

When switching from small group discussions to the whole class discussion, it sometimes helps to split the groups up and have them go back to their individual seats for the whole class discussion. If the students sit in the same small groups that they were in when they were encouraged to talk, they subconsciously think it is okay to just continue talking to those group members even though the teacher wants everyone listening to one speaker during the whole class discussion.

Strategy for Quick Transition: Timer and Marbles

I learned this one from Jennifer Tuttle, who teaches 6th grade at Durham School of the Arts in Durham, NC. This is a good strategy to use when you ask your students to transition from individual seating arrangements to group seating, or from a small group seating arrangement to a whole class discussion. If you need to give your students a little bit of time to move desks, get materials, or return materials, yet you do not want it to last too long, this is a good way to get them to transition quickly.

Here is how it works. Give the students directions for what you want them to do and then give the signal to move. Once you give the signal, set the time on a stopwatch for a reasonable period of time, perhaps 1 or 2 minutes—whatever amount of time you believe is reasonable. If everyone is in their place and ready to go before time is up, put a marble in the jar. Once the jar is full, the class gets a reward of your choosing. Ten minutes on Friday to talk about whatever they want with whomever they want might be just the trick. Or perhaps they get to eat popcorn one day while discussing the novel the class is reading.

Strategy for requesting teacher help: Red Cup/Green Cup

This small group strategy gives students an alternative to repeatedly calling out the teacher's name when their group needs help. Each group has two cups stacked on top of each other in the middle of their table. If the green cup is on top, that signals to the teacher that the group is working fine and no assistance is needed. However, the red cup on top signals to the teacher that the group is struggling and needs assistance as soon as the teacher becomes available. While the group is waiting on the teacher, they try to figure out their answer using techniques such as referring back to the text and rereading the section that may apply to the question.

Strategy for students helping each other first: Ask 3 before Me

This is a good strategy for fostering independence for small groups in middle grades who are discussing a challenging question. Often students faced with a tough challenge turn to the teacher too quickly to help them out. This strategy requires students to lean on each other before looking to the teacher for help. The procedure is: if a student is stumped or confused about how to proceed, that student must ask 3 other students for help before asking the teacher. Often, other students can clear up the confusion, and the teacher's assistance isn't needed. The strategy's value lies in its (1) requirement for students to work with each other, (2) lessening their dependence on the teacher, and (3) encouragement of students to use all of the resources available to them, an important life skill.

Strategy for one student dominating discussion: 3 Tallies

And then there is Roger, who was reading Wikipedia before he cut his first teeth. He knows the answer to everything (just ask him) and has an opinion on everything. He has never had an unexpressed thought. How do you keep one or two Rogers from dominating either small group or whole class discussions?

First, establish that it is not okay for Roger to dominate, even if he is saying correct, insightful things. The other students in the class need the opportunity to share their thoughts and if you allow Roger to continue, they will eventually shut down, leaving you and Roger to talk alone. Furthermore, Roger's behavior will hurt him in the future—no one wants to be around a person who tells everyone how much he knows all the time. It is in Roger's best interest to learn how to temper his contributions.

There are two parts to the solution for this problem. The first part of the solution is for you not to reinforce Roger. Perhaps, and this is just a hunch, you have been calling on Roger and allowing him to contribute more because he always knows the correct answer, which makes you feel good—as if you have done a good job teaching. And, if Roger knows the correct answer, then everyone else must know it, right? Wrong. Sometimes as teachers we tend to want to hear the correct answer repeated back to us, so we call on whoever will give it to us. It is within your power to stop this. Take control of the discussion and simply do not let Roger speak every time he wants to.

The second and equally important part of the solution lies within Roger. Remember, it is in the middle level years that we want students to begin establishing independence, but with guidance and structure. Some students need more scaffolding than others. When other students are not around, have a conference with Roger. Tell him that you are impressed with how hard he works and how eager he is to share in class. You appreciate his motivation. But also share with him the importance of learning from his classmates and letting them have their turns. Help him to understand that everyone's voice is important. Then teach him a self-regulating strategy. Tell him to make a tally mark at the top of his page every time he contributes in class. He is allowed two tally marks per class period. He is allowed a third only if the thought is so compelling that it cannot be contained. But that is it. No more than 3 tally marks per class period. He is always welcome to write down thoughts and hand them to you as he leaves the classroom.

Behavior management system: Classdojo.com

Classdojo.com is an Internet application that can be used on the class computer and displayed on the board. It also has a mobile app. This behavior management system allows the teacher to assign names to icons and give those icons points. You can use this to enhance group discussions by assigning groups to the icons. You can reward a group points for any behavior you wish to encourage. Some examples:

- Listening well to the ideas of others
- Coming up with a new idea as a group
- Being able to identify reasons for the other point of view
- Using textual evidence to support opinions
- Suggesting an alternative viewpoint tactfully

As you are giving points during the discussion, you can let the group know why they earned a point in order to reinforce the behavior, unless doing so would detract from their discussion. Class Dojo will give you a report that says what the groups earned points for, so you can pass this along to the groups allowing them to see what collaboration skills they are doing well on and which ones they need more work on. I wouldn't suggest using this data as a grade, but I would suggest some sort of a reward for the group with the most points. One possibility is that the group with the most points gets to select whether they will share first, middle, or last during the whole class presentation. Or you might give each member a "high five" ticket.

Strategy for encouraging certain behaviors: High Fives

This strategy comes from Dr. LuAnn Jordan who supervised my student teaching. It worked then, and still works today. High Fives are paper tickets that you create and then give to students for behaviors you wish to encourage such as answering a particularly challenging question. You can determine what High Fives can be traded for. High Fives come in handy when you want to push students past what they believe they are capable of. Thinking is hard work, and sometimes early adolescents need a little extra encouragement to do it.

Strategy for de-escalating

But what do you do for the extreme or combative comments that most often occur when the topic is controversial or particularly close to home? What about the student who wants to argue for argument's sake or who is antagonistic? Here are some responses you can use and that you can train your students to use.

- First, stay calm and use a calming tone of voice.

- Acknowledge the student's right to have an opinion, but remind the student to state it in an appropriate manner. Demonstrate how he or she could have said it.

- Restate the topic, stay on the issue, and resist responding to the emotion. Reframe the issue. For example, "It is important to hear Juan's concerns. What are the implications of ...(restate the question at hand).

- Resist taking the bait. You do not have to reply to every comment or question. However, it is not OK to ignore demeaning comments at any time.

- Use "I" messages, which leave room for discussion of the situation and consequences of actions. Instead of saying, "You are wrong!" say things such as, "I see what you mean," or "I can tell how frustrating this must be," or "I can see that you feel strongly about this," or "I hear your point of view."

- Acknowledge the speaker's feelings and offer empathy without agreeing or disagreeing. Try to determine the underlying motive for the statement and acknowledge it. "You really sound mad, upset, frustrated, disappointed, etc." "It is true that the 8th grade does not have a lot of free time between classes. Let's think about what Lisa said before that."

- Redirect the conversation back to the point you want to focus on. Here are helpful prompts:
  - That's another problem. Let's stay with this one.
  - You've presented some strong arguments for ____. Now what would happen if ____?
  - Another point that popped into my mind was____.

- Let's take a moment to focus on the good points. What idea appeals to you the most?
- The focus so far is _____. Is there anything else?
- Let's try this... _____
- Please consider_____.
- Let's put that issue on our flipchart for a separate discussion.

Troubleshooting Strategies for Management Problems

Discussion Problem	Strategy
One or two students dominate the discussion.	3 Tallies
The class just gets too loud.	Word on the Board Too Noisy App Have a Signal
Students are engaged in off-topic conversations.	10-15 Minute Rule Alternative Assignment Class Dojo Back to Individual Seats
They will answer the easy questions, but I have trouble motivating them to tackle the tough ones.	Ask 3 Before Me High Fives
Transitions take too long.	Timer and Marbles Class Dojo
Students argue with each other.	Alternative Assignment Class Dojo
I have trouble getting the class's attention when they are talking in small groups.	Word on the Board Have a Signal
My students interrupt each other or don't listen to each other.	Start with Partners Class Dojo High Fives

Conclusion

Managing a room full of middle level students during group discussions is challenging on the best day, with the best group of students. But it is well worth the effort. Give yourself and your students time to develop these skills. Be patient. Do not expect them to be perfectly behaved every day. If the first time you try to have a class discussion ends in chaos, don't give up. Reflect and try to determine what went wrong and how you might improve it the next time. Continue to communicate your expectations to your students. Ask other teachers or administrators to observe you and give you advice. Keep at it.... your students will benefit in the end.

Chapter 5
Whole Class Structures for Discussions

When I began using strategies for whole class discussions with young adolescents, I found that two factors are essential for success: variety and structure. Both are needed. This chapter will provide you with nine different strategies that provide structure for whole-class discussions. Rotating through these strategies allows you to have the variety that your students crave and will keep them more engaged. Any of the types of questions discussed in Chapter 2 would work for all of these strategies. As much as possible I have credited the original author of the strategy, but most have been significantly modified over time. These are intended to be generic templates, so you can modify any of the structures to fit your purposes. In other words, make the strategy work for the question(s) you are asking and for the group you are working with. In Chapter 6 I have included content examples from across the disciplines to model applying the strategies.

My graduate students use ring binders of cards with the various strategies and the steps for each. They flip through them to ensure that they are using different strategies regularly and not getting in the habit of using the same ones over and over again. For templates of the cards with these strategies go to Appendix E and amle.org/GettingThemtoTalk.

Speed Dating

Overview

The Speed Dating strategy (Murphy, 2005) was named after the popular dating concept. Speed Dating in the real world allows you to have short conversations with a variety of people during the course of an evening to determine with whom you would like to spend more time. If it makes you feel more comfortable, you could call it speed chatting. This classroom strategy spins that idea to partner students up for 2-minute conversations before moving them to a new partner. A benefit of this strategy is that it allows students to have conversations and hear the ideas of multiple students in the classroom, which is developmentally appropriate, as is the movement and change of the activity. Another benefit is that the strategy requires students to listen to their partners for one minute, giving them much-needed practice in this skill. Less-outspoken students can share their thoughts without being interrupted, and everyone has rehearsal time for articulating their ideas before the whole class discussion. Students with language issues get to hear more fluent peers modeling content vocabulary appropriately.

Step-by-Step

1. Pair students up in two rows of desks, with the desks facing each other and each student seated in a desk facing his or her partner. For example, in the diagram below Student A is paired with Student G for the first round.

Desk Facing Front	Student A	Student B	Student C	Student D	Student E	Student F
Desk Face Back	Student G	Student H	Student I	Student J	Student K	Student L

Desk Facing Front	Student M	Student N	Student O	Student P	Student Q	Student R
Desk Facing Back	Student S	Student T	Student U	Student V	Student W	Student X

2. The teacher poses a question on the board.

3. Students facing the front wall have one minute to answer the question, while their partners who are facing the back wall take notes of important points their partner shares. The partner facing the back wall can only listen and take notes without speaking for the entire minute. The students do not need to turn the notes in; the notes are simply an aid to help them organize their thinking about the most important points.

4. After one minute, the students switch roles (but stay seated in the same position). Students facing the back will answer the question for one minute while the students facing the front take notes.

5. Students facing the front all slide down one seat, while the students facing the back stay in their same position. For example, student A moves to where student B was seated, student B moves to where student C was seated, and so on. Student F moves to where student A was seated. This means every student now has a new partner.

6. The process repeats itself with new partners.

7. You can determine how many pairings you wish to have. Every student does not need to be paired with every other student. For example, if you want the Speed Dating process to last for about 6 minutes, then that would mean the students would work with 3 different pairs.

8. The process concludes with a whole class discussion in which the teacher asks the same questions and asks students to share ideas they heard from their various partners.

Tips

1. Use a timer such as online-stopwatch.com or a classroom timer to make it easy to measure the one-minute mark. Use something that has some kind of a ringer or bell that gets the students' attention and lets them know it is time to stop talking.

2. Spread the desks as far apart as possible to make it easier for students to hear their partners.

3. Alternate between whether the students facing the front wall or the students facing the back wall are the first to answer the question for each new round.

4. Each time the students move seats, you may consider asking the same question again or asking a new question. The benefit of asking the same question encourages students to refine their answers as they listen to different partners or to go deeper as they hear new ideas from multiple people.

5. Before switching to a new question, have a short class discussion in which individual students share ideas that they heard a partner say.

6. Allow the students to have their textbooks and/or notes open to use as references while answering the questions.

7. For an odd number of students, a different student sits out each round. Or the odd student can be paired with the teacher.

8. The whole class discussion at the end is the critical piece of this process. It gives the teacher the opportunity to pull together the key ideas he or she wants to address. The "speed dating" portion helps students form their thoughts and organize them.

Fishbowl

Overview

When you read through the Fishbowl strategy (Harris, 2011) that follows, think of people standing around an aquarium and observing what the fish inside are doing. The fish do not seem to be aware of their observers and are not concerned about who is watching them. They are busy going about their business and interactions with each other. The benefit of using this strategy is that it requires students outside the fishbowl to really listen since they are not currently participating in the discussion. The listening and note-taking give them the opportunity to refine their thinking and prepare for their own turn at sharing, which particularly helps reluctant speakers and those who struggle with language.

Step-by-Step

1. The class is divided into two groups: an inner circle called the "fish" and an outer circle called the "spectators".

2. The teacher poses a question on the board.

3. Those in the inner circle have 5 minutes to engage in dialogue about the question.

4. Only the fish in the inner circle may talk. The spectators in the outer circle will silently observe and take notes. They can take notes in whatever format they wish, but the goal is for them to record important ideas.

5. The two groups switch positions. The fish become spectators and the spectators become fish.

Tips

1. The teacher can choose to play the role of spectator or fish depending on the ability of the students to facilitate their own conversations.

2. The time can be adjusted based on the level of the question and the ability of the students to facilitate their own conversations.

3. You may wish to use a timer for this, or you may choose just to allow the discussion to run its course until you feel it has reached a good stopping place.

To see an example of another version of Fishbowl, see the link for a video in Appendix D.

Think Pair Share

Overview

This tried-and-true strategy can work for any type of question and can be incorporated quickly within any lesson. It is a good way to break up other longer activities. It is also a perfect activity for the reflective thinker who needs a little time to organize his/her thoughts. It gets every student in the room involved in conversation, so everyone's voice is heard. An advantage of this strategy is that it gives the students time to find evidence in the text to support whatever response they come up with to the question posed.

Step-by-Step

1. The teacher poses a question on the board.

2. *Think.* Each student thinks quietly for a moment about his or her answer to the question. The students write down their individual thoughts.

3. *Pair.* When the teacher feels that enough time has lapsed, the students share their ideas with a partner. Both partners take notes of the new ideas that they heard from the other.

4. *Share.* The teacher calls on students to share their thoughts with the class.

Tips

1. Having pre-assigned partners (such as elbow partners) who regularly pair up for this strategy is helpful. You don't want to have to assign partners every time you incorporate this strategy.

2. You may wish to use a timer for this, or you may just use your own judgment in pacing the steps by observing the conversations of the students.

3. Tell the students to find evidence from the text for their responses during the "think" and "pair" times.

Give One Get One

Overview

The Give One Get One strategy (Kagan & Kagan, 2009) requires students to get ideas from multiple students, not just their best friends. This strategy is a good way to summarize all of the key points of a chapter, unit, or big idea. The strategy also has a fringe benefit of allowing students to get up and move around the classroom. Students are under less pressure during the whole class discussion at the end when students share something from their paper since they may share something a classmate said and not necessarily their own idea. This works great for getting students to participate who are normally reluctant to share their own thoughts.

Step-by-Step

1. The teacher poses a question on the board.

2. Each student writes down his or her own ideas, based on the text or other information provided to the students in response to the question.

3. When students have had sufficient time to write down their ideas, the teacher asks them to circulate around the room.

4. Each student must share one idea with someone and collect an idea from him or her.

5. Then the student goes to a different person and repeats the process. Give one idea and get one idea.

6. A student may not collect more than one idea from any one person.

7. If a student finds a person who has the same idea written down, the two students must work together to come up with a new idea.

8. Each student is required to collect 4 new ideas.

9. Once all the students have their collection of ideas, the teacher begins the whole class discussion by asking students to share ideas from their lists. The whole class discussion allows the class to compile a master list of the key ideas that were important in the chapter or unit.

Tips

1. You can change the number of new ideas they are required to collect depending on the question and the time you have available.

2. You may consider using a timer to help students remain focused and on-task. If they know there is a time limit, they will be less likely to wander.

3. The whole class discussion at the end is the critical piece of this process. It gives the teacher the opportunity to pull together the key ideas he or she wants to address. The give one, get one portion helps students form their thoughts and organize them.

5. During the whole class discussion, the teacher helps the class synthesize or analyze the information based on the original discussion question and goals for the lesson. The teacher might ask the class to look for themes in the lists, or he might ask the students to compare and contrast two ideas. The teacher and class can determine how best to organize the information to make sense of it and to answer the key question.

Snowball Fight

Overview

What student wouldn't love to throw paper in class with your permission? The Snowball Fight strategy (Harris, 2011) has the advantage of adding energy to your classroom and allowing students to get up and move. This strategy is exactly what its name says it is, a good old-fashioned snowball fight, with some structure, of course. An additional benefit to this strategy is that it requires students to add thoughts to what previous students said, so they will go beyond the surface-level response, which is one of the Common Core Comprehension and Collaboration standards. Students are encouraged to use their text or class notes to add more information to the comments of their classmates. In effect, this gives students a chance to rehearse what they will say in the whole class discussion giving them confidence and content to share. Because they are sharing something a classmate has written and not necessarily their own ideas, it is especially beneficial for getting students to participate who are normally reluctant to share their own thoughts.

Step-by-Step

1. Every student writes his/her name at the top of a clean sheet of paper.

2. The teacher poses a question and each student writes down an idea or answer.

3. Once students have been given sufficient time to write their responses, the teacher asks everyone to crumple up their paper and throw it ONCE.

4. Each student picks up a new "snowball" from the floor. They then respond to or add to what the person before them wrote.

5. The process repeats.

6. When the teacher decides the snowball fight should end, the students return their papers to the original owners. The teacher leads a whole class discussion, asking students to share ideas from their snowballs.

7. The whole class discussion at the end is the critical piece of this process. It gives the teacher the opportunity to pull together the key ideas to address. The snowball portion helps students form their thoughts and organize them.

8. If you want to use the snowballs as formative assessment data, have students write their names beside the comments.

Airplane Questions

Overview

This novel way to begin a discussion easily adapts to any type of question, since you are posing a question for the students to consider, just not in a traditional format such as a worksheet or textbook. The benefit of this strategy is that it allows for physical movement of the students, which is a critical need for early adolescents. I recommend you use this strategy sparingly, because it uses precious class time to allow students to make their airplanes.

Step-by-Step

1. Each student writes a question on a clean sheet of paper. The questions could originate from a textbook, worksheet, or the teacher can pose them.

2. Each student folds his or her question into a paper airplane.

3. Airplanes are thrown one at a time. The student closest to where the airplane lands is the first to respond to the question. The teacher then facilitates a class discussion encouraging other students to add to the first student's response. The process is repeated until all responses are discussed.

Tips

1. To add a little fun and excitement, you could offer a prize to the plane that flies the best or the farthest.

2. You can limit the number of questions on the airplanes by giving the same question to multiple students in the classroom.

3. You might also consider printing the questions on paper ahead of time. This is helpful if you want to limit the number of questions. For example, if you have only 4 questions you want to ask and you have a class of 24 students, you can print 6 copies of each question and pass them out to the class.

Chain Note

Overview

The benefit of the Chain Note strategy (Angelo & Cross, 1993) is that it requires students to respond in multiple ways. In other words, you cannot repeat the answer someone else in your group gave. You must either go deeper or broader. The strategy encourages students to dig deeper and not just scratch the surface with an easy response. Although it began as an assessment strategy, I believe it works well to get good discussions going. It is an ideal strategy for those reflective students who need a little time to think before they share with the whole class.

Step-by-Step

1. The teacher arranges the students into rows or groups of equal numbers (For example, 6 groups of 5 students).

2. The teacher has questions prepared based on the number of students in each group. For example, if there are 5 students in each group, then the teacher has 5 different questions prepared. Each question is written at the top of a sheet of paper.

3. The teachers passes the sheets out so that each student in each group gets one of the 5 different questions.

4. The students individually answer the question that they have been given in writing.

5. After a sufficient amount of time has passed, the teacher asks the students to pass their papers down the row or to the next person in the group.

6. The students then add something new to what the person before them wrote.

7. The process repeats until everyone has answered all 5 questions. Once this has been done, the teacher leads a whole class discussion about each of the questions.

Tips

1. Consider printing the questions on different colored sheets of paper. That will help you track the progress of the chain notes and also eliminates confusion about which question is being discussed by the whole group. "Let's talk about the blue question now…"

2. When students share something from their papers, they are under less stress because they are sharing something a group member said and not necessarily their own ideas. This works great for getting students to participate who are normally reluctant to share their own thoughts.

3. The whole class discussion at the end is the critical piece of this process. It gives the teacher the opportunity to pull together the key ideas he or she wants to address. The chain note portion helps students form their thoughts and organize them.

4. If you want to use the chain notes as formative assessment data, have students write their names beside the comments.

Select a Passage

Overview

This strategy is best used when you want depth instead of breadth. It gives students some ownership of the direction of the discussion and the ideas that they believe are the most important to talk about. It is important for middle grades students to see relevance in the curriculum and to make connections to ideas important to them. It works best when the text has ideas that are open for interpretation or opinions.

Step-by-Step

1. Students individually select a passage from the text that stood out to them in some way. It could be something they agreed with, or something they thought was confusing. It might be something they found interesting or something that was a new idea to them. The students are allowed to set their own criteria for selecting the passage.

2. The teacher calls on students to read the passage they selected and share the reason for selecting the specific passage. The teacher encourages other students to elaborate or add to the thoughts of the original student who shared the passage (building on the ideas of others is the first collaboration standard).

3. When subsequent students are called on, they must select a different passage to discuss.

Tips

1. Be sure to require students to share the rationale for selecting the passage. "I just liked it" does not count. Make them back up their opinions with evidence.

2. Have your own passages selected and marked in case an important idea is not raised in the discussion. You can then share the passage covering that idea.

Beach Ball

Overview

This strategy is the perfect way to add energy and excitement to your classroom. It can be adapted to different types of questions depending on your purpose and it has the added benefit of allowing physical movement in the classroom which is critical for early adolescents. Any of the types of questions discussed in Chapter 2 can be written on the ball. The beach ball strategy simply gives a novel way to pose a question, rather than just reading the question in a textbook or worksheet. The question is posed using the beach ball and then the whole class discusses the question beginning with the student who caught the ball.

Step-by-Step

1. Write questions across the surface of a cheap plastic inflatable ball.

2. The teacher throws the ball to one student. When a student catches the ball, he or she must answer the question closest to the tip of their right index finger. The teacher facilitates as the whole class continues discussion of the question.

3. When the teacher determines it is time to move on to the next question, he or she asks the student to throw the ball to another student.

Tips

1. Questions could be general prompts that would fit any text such as, "What I learned was..." "One question I have is...." "The main idea of the story was....", or they could be specific questions about the particular reading.

2. You could put the numbers 1-5 on the ball that correspond to the 5 questions on a worksheet or the 5 questions you have projected on the screen at the front of the room.

3. Use a dry-erase marker. This allows you to remove the questions at the end and start with a clean ball for the next discussion.

4. You may want to establish a rule that only the person with the ball in his or her hands may speak. If you choose to do this, you will want to have students toss the ball during the discussion of each question, instead of just throwing the ball when it is time for the next question. You can just announce when you are ready to move to the next question. In other words, 6-7 students may have caught the ball during the discussion of Question 1 and then a different 5 students may have caught the ball during the discussion of Question 2, and so on.

Chapter 6
Examples of Class Talk

To show how these strategies might actually play out in a class discussion, in this chapter I have illustrated how using several of them might support student learning of the content of various subjects. In addition, I have purposefully selected topics in science, math, and social studies to illustrate how discussions in these areas can support learning comprehension and collaboration standards that fall within the Common Core literacy standards. Students can develop collaboration skills in any subject, and those skills will further support the learning of the content.

Science Class Discussion

Content Objective—Students will be able to explain how structures of coniferous and deciduous trees relate to their environments.

National Science Standards C (E.C.1 b.) Each plant or animal has different structures that serve different functions in growth, survival, and reproduction.

Collaboration Objective—Students will be able to respond to the comments of other students and build on those ideas.

Key Concepts—

- Coniferous trees:
  - Seeds grow in cones
  - Small, stiff leaves
  - Needlelike or scale-like leaves
  - Grow in a triangular shape and upward rather than outward
  - Grow well in dry, cold climates because small leaves reduce need for water; thick cell walls reduce freezing; and leaves have less surface area for wind to dry them

- Deciduous trees:
  - Broad, flat leaves
  - Leaves/fruit only last one growing season
  - Leaves contain more water
  - Spread out as they grow to a round shape
  - Seeds grow in nuts or fruit
  - Grow in climates with a lot of seasonal variability because leaves fall off during winter

Overarching Question—How are the structures of coniferous and deciduous trees related to their environments?

Structure—Speed Dating

How the Speed Dating part of the discussion might work:

- With their first partner, the students discuss Question 1: What are the characteristics of coniferous trees? In this example, the teacher begins with a couple low-level questions to get all the facts on the table. It is fine for this discussion (and any discussion) for the students to have their resources in front of them such as the textbook, the class notes, another handout, or whatever resource might provide the content information to them.

- With their second partner, the students discuss Question 2: What are the characteristics of deciduous trees?

- With their third partner, the students discuss Question 3: How might the different characteristics reflect each plant's way of life? Because this is the "big" or overarching question for discussion, the teacher may have them switch to a fourth partner and discuss Question 3 again with their new partner.

At this point, the students should have a list of ideas they have written down for each of the 3 questions in their notes.

How the whole class discussion might work: The teacher creates a table on the board with 2 columns labeled Coniferous Trees and Deciduous Trees and calls on students to list as many characteristics as possible for each cell. As they share their ideas, one student fills in the table. The final table might look like this.

Tree Characteristics

Coniferous Trees	Deciduous Trees
Cones	Broad leaves
Small leaves	Flat leaves
Stiff leaves	Flexible leaves
Needlelike or scale like leaves	Leaves/fruit only last one growing season
Most are evergreens (keep leaves year-round)	Contain more water
Grow upward rather than outward	Spread out as they grow
Triangular shape	More rounded shape
Seeds grow in cones	Seeds grow in nuts or fruit
Softwoods	Hardwoods
Common examples: fir, pine, spruce	Common examples: oak, maple

After students have filled in the chart with facts they have gathered, the real work of the discussion begins. The teacher must lead students from the facts they have all gathered to the meaning of them. This is one of the most challenging aspects of teaching, as you have to maintain your focus on the goal you have for students while adjusting your pathway of getting there depending on what students share of their different thinking processes along the way. The teacher might begin by asking the students to look at the list of characteristics of coniferous trees and determine connections between those characteristics and the fact that they are generally found in dry climates and in colder regions. As the students offer suggestions, the teacher might lead them to connections and end up with something that looks like this on the board:

How are characteristics related to the trees' environments?

Coniferous Trees	Deciduous Trees
They are adapted to dry climates due to: Needlelike shape of leaves reduces water loss and sustains the life of the plant in dryer conditions. They are adapted to cold climates and mountainous regions with a lot of snow due to: 1. The narrow needles offer less surface area to the drying winds of winter. 2. The thick cell walls contain little water so they resist freezing. 3. The leaves photosynthesize year-round to provide enough food in cold climates with little sunlight. 4. The triangular shape of the trees allows heavy snow to slide off easily.	They are adapted to living in places where there are greater changes in seasonal temperatures due to: 1. The broad flat leaves catch a lot of light, which makes photosynthesis easier. 2. Cannot survive without warmth and water so the leaves turn colors and fall off in the winter. 3. The leaves contain lots of water; when they fall off, it reduces the demand on the tree to maintain its water balance, which is helpful in the winter when there is less water available in the soil. 4. Without their leaves, they can't produce food, and they stop growing during the winter.

Troubleshooting—The teacher needs to be aware of and address any misconceptions articulated by students that involve individual plants adapting during their life cycles to their environmental conditions. Although evolution isn't the focus of this discussion, it is a fundamental concept directly related, even if unexpressed.

Math Class Discussion

Content Objective—Students will be able to compare the steepness of the slope of two lines when represented in different forms.

Common Core State Standards.Math.Content.8.F.A.2 Compare properties of two functions each represented in a different way (algebraically, graphically, numerically in tables, or by verbal descriptions).

Collaboration Objective—Students will demonstrate they understand the ideas of others by paraphrasing those ideas.

Key Concepts—

- The slope represents the steepness of a line, or its rate of change
- In the form y = mx + b, m represents the slope
- In the graph of a line, slope can be determined by computing rise/run
- In a table, the slope of the line can be determined by finding the difference in the Ys, if the difference in the Xs is constant at 1.

Overarching Question—How can you tell which line will be steeper if you have two lines represented in different forms?

Structure—Chain Note

How the Chain Note part of the discussion might work:

The teacher arranges the students into groups of 4. Each student in each group of 4 receives a different one of the 4 chain notes listed below on a sheet similar to the example in Table 6-1.

Chain Note #1: Represent the line that goes through the coordinates (0, 1) and (2, 3) in 3 different ways. The first person draws the graph, the second person makes a table, the third person writes the equation, and the fourth person records the slope of the line.

Chain Note #2: Represent the line that goes through the coordinates (0, 1) and (2, 5) in 3 different ways. The first person draws the graph, the second person makes a table, the third person writes the equation, and the fourth person records the slope of the line.

Chain Note #3: Represent the line that goes through the coordinates (0, 1) and (2, 7) in 3 different ways. The first person draws the graph, the second person makes a table, the third person writes the equation, and the fourth person records the slope of the line.

Chain Note #4: Represent the line that goes through the coordinates (0, 1) and (1, 1) in 3 different ways. The first person draws the graph, the second person makes a table, the third person writes the equation, and the fourth person records the slope of the line.

Table 6-1

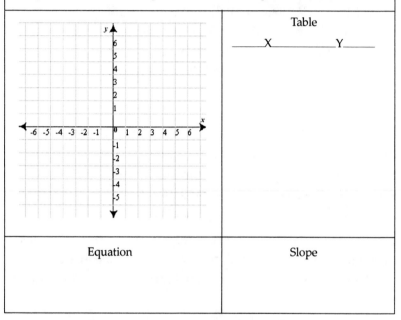

Chain Note #1
Represent the line that goes through the coordinates (0, 1) and (2, 3) in 3 different ways. The first person draws the graph, the second person makes a table of at least 5 coordinates, the third person writes the equation, and the fourth person records the slope of the line.

	Table
	_____X_____Y_____
Equation	Slope

The teacher sets a timer and gives the students an appropriate amount of time (approximately 1-2 minutes) to complete the first step of their chain note. This means that all 4 students of a given group are now drawing a graph of a line going through the two coordinates, but each of the 4 students will have a different line on their paper, because they were given different coordinates than the rest of their group members.

When the timer rings, the students pass their papers clockwise and each student now has a different line to work with. Again, the teacher sets the timer, and this time each student makes a table of at least 5 coordinates included in the line.

When the timer rings, the papers are passed clockwise again and now each sheet of paper is in the hands of the third student to work on it. The teacher resets the timer and now, every student is writing an equation for the line represented on their paper.

For the final leg in the chain note, each student determines the slope of the line for the last paper. At this point, each sheet of paper will have made it around to each member of the group so that every student has done some representation or work on each of the 4 linear equations.

How the whole class discussion might work:

Now the teacher brings the students' attention together as a whole class. I recommend using four colors of pen on the Smartboard, one for each line, staying consistent with the same color for all three representations of each line. The teacher would ask students to share portions of the information on their chain notes and while asking the students to share their work, records those answers on the board. In the end the board might look something like this:

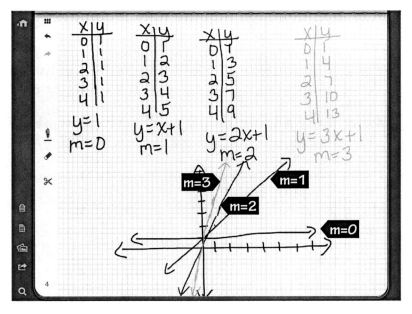

Now is where the real work of the discussion can begin. The teacher poses the question, "How can you tell which line will be steeper if you have two lines represented in different forms?" The discussion might go like this:

Teacher: (after pausing a few moments to allow students time to think) I want to make sure everyone understands my question. Tia, can you rephrase what I am asking?

Tia: You mean, like for example, if you had the table for a line and the equation for another line. Or you had the graph for a line and the coordinates for a different line. How could you tell which would be steeper?

Teacher: Give me a thumbs up if you understand the question. (Everyone responds). Okay, so let's get some ideas on the board. Who has a thought to get us started?

John: Well you can tell by looking at these 4 equations that the bigger the number the slope is, the steeper it is.

Teacher: Laura, can you explain what John just said?

Laura: Yeah, I agree with him. When the slope was 0, the line was flat. When it was 1, it was a little steeper. When it was 2, it was a little steeper. The steepest line has the largest slope, which is 3. So the steepest lines have the largest slopes and the flattest lines have the smallest slopes.

Karif: Yeah, it's real easy to tell when you have the number for the slope. Whichever number is biggest, that's the steepest slope.

Teacher: Okay, one idea that we can write down in our notes, and I will write on the board at the same time, is that the larger the slope, the steeper the line. (gives students time to write down the idea)

Teacher: But what if I don't have the number for the slope? We have all the slopes lined up nice and neat here, but what if like Tia said, I just had the table for one line and the equation for another line? Or something like that? How could I tell which had the steepest slope?

Manuel: Well, you could graph both of them and just look at which is steeper.

Teacher: Okay, that is another idea that I will write down on the board. Does everyone agree, or does anyone disagree? (no one disagrees)

Ashley: It's like you can't compare apples and oranges. You got to get them to the same thing. Either they both have to be graphs, or they both have to be tables, or they both have to be equations.

Teacher: Let's write the idea on our list. Someone give me a short way to say what Ashley just said.

Leo: Turn them into the same form.

Shante: But I disagree. I don't think you have to get them to the same representation.

Teacher: Okay, explain what you mean.

Shante: You don't have to have them in the same form, you just have to know what the slope is. I can tell the slope of line m=0 by just looking at the differences in the y's in the table. And I can tell the slope of the equation of line m=3 by just looking at the number in front of x in its equation. I know the first table's slope is 0 and the last line's slope is 3. That's a lot less trouble than having to graph them both.

Teacher: So, Shante's idea is to find the slope of both lines. Let's write that idea down.

Teacher: Does anyone else have any other ideas? (No one responds).

Teacher: Well, I think it is important to remember how to find the slope of each form, so let's add that to our list of ideas.....

The class goes on to write the method for finding the slope in each representation. It would also be important for the teacher to raise the issue of a negative slope if a student doesn't and to lead the class in a discussion of what this does to the "steepness of the line" idea that they have suggested.

Social Studies Class Discussion

> **Content Objective**—Students will cite evidence from text to analyze how point of view shapes the content of a speech.
>
> Common Core Standards.ELA-Literacy.RH.6-8.1 Cite specific textual evidence to support analysis of primary and secondary sources.
>
> **Collaboration Objective**—The students will refer to evidence from the text to support their claims.
>
> **Key Concepts—**
>
> • The Persian Gulf War began after Iraq invaded Kuwait.
>
> • President Bush of the United States believed that reasonable diplomatic efforts had been taken to avoid the war, and the war was necessary to protect Kuwait.
>
> • King Hussein of Jordan believed the war could have been avoided with more diplomatic efforts and that Iraq was a victim of a cruel war by more powerful countries.
>
> **Overarching Question**—What were the different points of views of leaders of key countries regarding the necessity of the Persian Gulf War?

Structure—Give One, Get One

How the Give One, Get One part of the discussion might work:

Step 1: The students are given excerpts of two speeches, the first made by President Bush of the United States on January 16, 1991, and the second made by King Hussein of Jordan on February 6, 1991. The students are asked to read the two speeches and to write down what they believe the point of view of each leader was regarding whether or not the Persian Gulf War should have started. The teacher asks the class what the general position of the two leaders was and labels two columns on the board:

President Bush of the United States	King Hussein of Jordan
Believed the Persian Gulf War was justified	Believed the Persian Gulf War should have been avoided.

Step 2: Next, the students are asked to divide their paper into two columns, one for each leader, and list one piece of evidence from the text to support their claim about that leader's point of view.

Step 3: The students circulate around the room and find a person to partner with. To their first partner, they give an idea from one of their columns, and get one from their partner. Next, they find someone else in the class to share with. They give an idea to that person, and get an idea for either column. They continue this process until they have 3 different ideas in each column and then return to their seats.

How the whole class discussion might work:

Next the teacher writes on the board as many ideas as the students have to offer. As the teacher asks students to contribute ideas from their lists, she continually requires them to refer to specific evidence from the text. A portion of the discussion might sound like this:

> *Teacher:* James, give us one of the items of evidence that you have on your paper that supports the claim that President Bush believed the Persian Gulf War was justified.
>
> *James:* He acted like Kuwait was a victim.
>
> *Teacher:* Can you give us evidence from the speech?
>
> *James:* Yeah, he described Kuwait as a "small and helpless neighbor".
>
> *Keshaun:* It's interesting that King Hussein made Iraq look like the helpless one.
>
> *Teacher:* Back that up with evidence from the text, Keshaun.

Keshaun: He talked about all the things that were destroyed by the "biggest and most powerful nations", things like hospitals and powdered milk factories. He makes it sound like the big nations were bullies to helpless Iraqi citizens.

After continued discussion, the lists on the board might look like this:

President Bush of the United States	King Hussein of Jordan
Believed the Persian Gulf War was justified.	Believed the Persian Gulf War should have been avoided.
1. He described Kuwait as a victim: "small and helpless neighbor"	1. He described Iraq as a victim: the "biggest and most powerful nations" destroyed things like milk factories and hospitals.
2. He claimed long-term diplomatic efforts: "months of constant and virtually endless diplomatic activity"	2. He claimed there wasn't enough diplomatic effort: "all the good offices of Jordan and others… were [cut short]."
3. He said Arab leaders sought an "Arab solution."	3. He said the Arab parties rejected "any political Arab dialogue with Iraq"
4. He said the purpose of the war was to "drive Saddam from Kuwait."	4. He said the purpose of the war was to "destroy Iraq and rearrange the area."

Following that, the teacher asks the students how the point of view of each leader impacted the rhetoric of their speech. The discussion might go like this:

Teacher: So how did the point of view of each leader impact their speech?

Caitlyn: Well, President Bush made a lot of effort to show that they had really tried to avoid the war and he seemed to be justifying it. He talked about the "endless diplomatic activity" and that the United Nations was involved, not just the United States.

Teacher: Can anyone add to what Caitlyn said?

Nai: Well he also talked about how Arab leaders were involved and how people traveled to Baghdad to try to prevent it. He kept emphasizing how hard we tried to avoid it. He used phrases like "exhausted all reasonable efforts" and "have no choice but to drive Saddam out."

Teacher: Then how did King Hussein's point of view shape his speech?

Njeri: Well he kept emphasizing how the war wasn't justified and made it sound like the Coalition forces were just mean. He talked about how bad it was for Iraq and how it could have been avoided if the other countries had tried harder.

Teacher: What are phrases that he used to evoke sympathy for Iraq and to make the Coalition forces seem "mean"?

Njeri: He talked about "Fire raining down upon Iraq" and how the powerful nations "unleashed their modern and dangerous weapons."

Using the Give One, Get One discussion strategy to analyze the point of view of two different political leaders also supports student learning of the important social studies content. For examples of class talk that models encouraging student interactions with each other that move responsibility for clarification from teachers to students, see Appendix B, "Encouraging Students to Engage in Class Discussions."

Chapter 7
Grouping for Talk

The reality is that if you want students to engage in rich discussions, you can't do just whole class discussions. Because the teacher is in control during whole class discussions, the method can prevent students from taking charge of their own learning, and student choice is important at the middle school level. Another disadvantage of whole class discussions is the number of "at bats" (Lemov, 2010) any given student can have. Students simply don't get the opportunity to speak as much if they are 1 of 28 people all taking turns rather than if they are 1 of 4 in a group. In small groups students have the power and responsibility to direct the path of the discussion and therefore, their learning.

One of the most important reasons for working in small groups is that they serve as a precursor to the whole class discussion. This gives reflective thinkers a few minutes to put their thoughts together and ruminate before they articulate their ideas to the larger group. Many early adolescents have low self-esteem and benefit from building their confidence by sharing their ideas with a few others before they share them with the whole class. In small groups students try out ideas and collect, organize, and refine their thoughts before engaging in the whole class discussion (McCann, Johannessen, Kahn, & Flanagan, 2006).

Size of Small Groups

To begin working with groups, first decide the size of the groups. Several factors affect this decision such as the number of materials that you have available and the complexity of the task. If students are engaging in an involved project, working in groups of 4 allows them to divide the labor and generate more ideas. However, if the lesson requires just a quick discussion using a strategy such as Think, Pair, Share, groups of two may suffice.

Important point: The maximum number of students in a group is four—more than 4 middle graders working together need adult intervention. If you have more than four, students will begin working in subgroups rather than one whole group. A group of 5 can work occasionally in a classroom of students who have experience working well together, but that is the exception, not the rule. Once I observed a classroom with students working in groups of 8. Each group wrote their ideas with an overhead marker on a single transparency sheet. Because not every student could see the transparency, the group lost focus and there were too many different ideas and opinions flying around at the same time.

Types of Small Groups

There are basically three ways to arrange groups: the teacher assigns the groups, the students select their own groups, or the groups are randomly arranged. Teachers can assign students to groups that are heterogeneous or homogeneous based on ability. Figure 7-1 shows the possible arrangements.

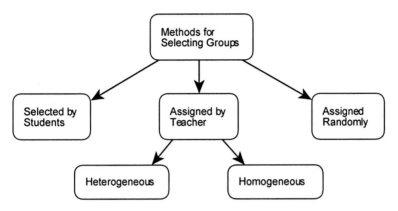

Figure 7-1: Methods for Selecting Groups

There are pros and cons to each type of group, and there are times when one of these choices is preferable to the others. I suggest that the teacher consider all of the options for any given lesson and select the one best suited for that lesson. Let's look at the pros, cons, and some tips for each method.

Students Select Their Own Groups

Pros

- Provides autonomy and choice; fosters independence
- Creates harmonious climate with less arguing; increases on-task behavior
- Provides leverage for teacher ("If you stay on-task, you may choose whom you work with today.")

Cons

- Provides opportunity for unwise decisions
- Allows for student(s) to be left out and then "forced" on a group
- Increases monitoring for off-topic conversations among friends

Tips

- Set a timer. Give the students 2 minutes to select their groups, arrange their desks, prepare the materials, and begin the task. Any student who is not able to complete this in 2 minutes works alone. If you are consistent in applying this rule, believe me, they soon learn that they are capable of doing all this in 2 minutes.

Assigned By the Teacher: Heterogeneous Ability Groups

Pros

- Stronger students can support weaker students.
- Weaker students benefit by listening to the vocabulary of stronger students.
- This represents common real-world scenarios in which we usually find ourselves working with people who are different from us. This gives students experience and practice at successfully working with people of different skill levels.

Cons

- Research has shown that weaker students benefit in these arrangements, but gifted students do not necessarily benefit (nor are they harmed) (Allan, 1991).
- You run the risk of the stronger students doing the majority of the talking or doing the thinking part, while lower-level students are relegated to more menial tasks.

Tips

- Assigning job responsibilities helps ensure that all students contribute to the work and are learning. For example, one group member is the researcher (finds the information), one is the analyzer (synthesizes the information), one is the developer (organizes the information), etc.

Assigned By the Teacher: Homogeneous Ability Groups

Pros

- This grouping is ideal for differentiation. Using data from a formative assessment, the teacher arranges students based on what they already know. Questions of different levels and complexities can be strategically asked of different groups.
- If everyone in the group is roughly of the same ability, than all of the members have to step up and contribute, rather than sitting back and allowing the higher-level students to do the thinking.

Cons

- If everyone in the group has a weak content vocabulary, there is no one to support this development.

Tips

- When leading the whole class discussion, begin with the weakest group that had the lowest-level question and work your way up to the highest-level group.
- The teacher can scaffold lower-level groups by spending more time in their proximity and interjecting comments into the conversation or by providing vocabulary sheets.

Assigned Randomly

Pros

- Allows students to hear viewpoints of people with whom they may not normally associate. In our global economy, it is increasingly more important to appreciate diversity with its multiple perspectives and differing points of view. A student who begins to learn how to hear and deal with a variety of viewpoints and not just the viewpoints of their few close friends will develop skills now that will benefit him/her throughout life.

- Erases the complaint that the teacher "has it out for them"; it was just the luck of the draw if a student ends up working with someone they don't like.

Cons

- Risks students with behavior issues ending up in the same group.

Tips

- Any teacher worth her salt has the ability to manipulate a random system as needed. For example, if you are grouping students using playing cards and you are going to put the aces together—the kings together, the queens, and the jacks, and so on—then, have the deck arranged that way. Pass the cards out at the door as students arrive. Friends will typically arrive in the classroom together because they were hanging out together in the hall. You can quickly make sure that one friend gets a jack, one friend gets an ace, and one friend gets a nine. If you know the system before the students do, then you can ensure that key students do not get the cards that will land them in the same group.

- Invoke the teacher veto and rearrange a couple groups if necessary. Require those who regularly lead each other astray to switch groups. Maintain the power of the teacher veto.

Strategies for Assigning Students to Groups

Spinning Wheel

Using cardstock, create three concentric circles of three different sizes (see Figure 7-2). Divide the class roll into three lists. One list is written around each of the three circles so that the names line up. Place a metal brad in the middle of the center circle to connect the three circles allowing them to turn. When the teacher spins the circles, the students who are lined up with each other work together.

The advantage of this strategy is that the teacher can manipulate the lists. For example, the teacher might decide to put all of the talkative students on the outer circle and all of the quiet students on the inner circle. This means that every group will end up with no more than one talkative student and one quiet student.

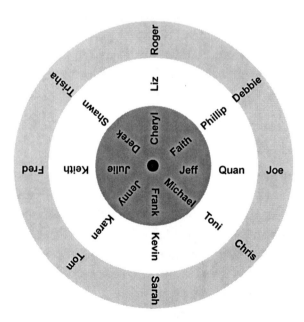

Figure 7-2: Spinning Wheel

Matching Plates

This is a fun way to incorporate movement and randomly assign students to groups. The teacher creates two sets of paper plates with items that match each other. Some of the many variations for the matching items are: vocabulary terms and definitions, questions and answers, and equations and solutions. The teacher randomly passes out the plates and the students find their matches. The students with whom they match become their partners for the discussion.

Playing Cards

As students enter the room, each student is given a playing card. When it's time for the discussion during the lesson, students work with the students of the same suit (all hearts together, spades together, etc.). Or, students could work with others of the same number (all jacks together, all sevens together, etc.). Another option is for the teacher to tell students to get into a run of four (jack, queen, king, ace, or three, four, five, six).

Candy Groups

A little chocolate goes a long way in making for a happy class. Pass a jar of mixed candy around the room and allow everyone to select one piece. There should be no more than four pieces of any type of candy in the jar. Then tell all of the Skittles to work together, the Butterfingers to work together, the Snickers to work together, etc. This is just a fun, different way to randomly assign students to groups.

2:00 Appointments

This is a quick way to regularly alternate partners. Instead of having students always discuss ideas with their elbow partner, have an appointment sheet for each student. At the beginning of the term give each student an appointment schedule. The schedule should have times of the day on it with a blank beside each time. Example:

9:00	_____
10:00	_____
11:00	_____
12:00	_____
1:00	_____

Students fill out their schedule by walking around the room and arranging appointments. If Sarah lists Holly as her 11:00 appointment, then Holly does the same on her sheet. This only needs to be done once at the beginning of the year and kept in students' notebooks.

When you want to have a discussion with partners, select a time and tell students to find their appointment for that time slot. For example, "Discuss this with your 1:00 appointment." (Hollas, 2007)

Random Generators

Use an app or the computer to create the groups for you. A couple options I've used are *List Selector* for iPads and the group maker tool at superteachertools.com and there are others.

After you enter the names from your class roll and specify how many groups you want, the computer randomly assigns the groups.

Guidelines for Small Groups

Working productively in small groups does not come naturally or automatically. A few simple guidelines will help students learn how to work productively in groups and what they should be doing when they are working together. At the beginning of the school year, discuss these as a class before your first small group discussion and then refer to them as necessary. Posting them on the wall will help reinforce them.

Work together on each question: Have them discover the value of synergy of ideas (the total effect is greater than the sum of the individual parts). You may want to take the time at the beginning of the year to have your students experience synergy through a group activity that may be loosely related to your content. Perhaps you bring in a bag of random items found in an historical figure's pocket at his death. The groups must come up with a plausible story of how the items got there. If the students write their ideas individually first and then compare them to the group's ideas, they will likely see that the group came up with a more interesting story.

The "Lost on the Moon" activity from NASA allows students to discover some principles for working effectively together as they compare the results of their problem solving done by (1) working alone (2) working as part of a group and voting, and (3) working as part of a group that actively seeks consensus. (see Appendix D).

Or you could try one of the hundreds of synergy activities suggested on the Internet. The point is to engage them in an exercise in creativity where they can experience synergy and discover the power of working in a group versus working individually. In other words, the whole is greater than the sum of its parts.

Tell your students that it is important that everyone in the group participates and shares their thoughts and ideas. It is not okay to sit back and be quiet and let the others do the thinking, but it is just as bad for one person to take over and make all the decisions. Both extremes will cause their group to be less successful problem solvers than if they learn to build on each other's ideas.

Brainstorming: If you are asking a question that requires students to come up with a new idea based on content they have learned, than brainstorming may be a good technique to start with. Teach students how to brainstorm in small groups by modeling this as a whole class from time to time. One brainstorming technique that can work well in small groups is to have everyone free write whatever comes to their minds individually for a couple minutes and then share their ideas with the group. Another brainstorming technique is to create a group list where everyone adds as many ideas as possible as quickly as possible without pausing for evaluation. No one is allowed to criticize or laugh at any of the ideas. Then after a few minutes, the group slows down and goes back and selects a few of the better ideas to explore.

Listen carefully to each other: This is a tough one for middle graders (and for adults, as well). We all tend to talk way, way more than we listen. Tell students that one of the main reasons to listen to others in their group is so that they can build on the ideas of others.

Achieve a group answer to each question: The goal of each group should be to come up with a group answer. In other words, tell the students to avoid writing their ideas in their own notebook and not coming up with what the group considers to be the best idea or ideas.

Make sure that everyone in the group can explain and justify the answer: Everyone in the group should be actively involved in the discussion and able to explain the conclusions of the group on the group's behalf. It should be a normal practice in the classroom that any student may be called on to speak for their group, so they should all be ready.

Student roles: You may find it helpful in the beginning to assign roles to students. If you do choose to assign roles, rotate these roles through the group members, so each day a given student plays a different role. Some potential roles are:

Leader—Responsible for starting the discussion, moving it along, and keeping it on-topic, the leader tries to get everyone to participate and ensures that no one dominates the discussion.

Pacer—Keeping an eye on the timer, the pacer moves the group along to complete the task by their deadline. For example, if the group has two questions to discuss in 10 minutes, the pacer can suggest that they finish up question 1 and begin moving to question 2 around the 5-minute mark.

Recorder—The recorder notes the groups' ideas on notebook paper, chart paper, or an electronic device so that they can be summarized and shared with the class during the whole class discussion. Creating a visual diagram of some sort is often helpful.

Collegiality monitor—If a group member violates one of the rules for collegial discussions established by the class and posted on the wall (see Chapter 4), the collegiality monitor politely gives a reminder of the rule.

Discuss these roles with the students and talk about the responsibilities of each role. Ask the students to come up with examples of successful, productive performances of each role by showing what does and doesn't work and why. For example:

Collegiality monitor:

Teacher: Let's say Hannah suggested that the group should solve the problem by listing the numbers in a table. And let's say another group member, who shall remain nameless, said, "That will never work!"

Teacher: An example of what a collegiality monitor should not do is this, "Don't criticize others!"

Teacher: An example of what a collegiality monitor should do is this, "Remember, if you disagree with someone, you should say so politely, give a reason, or ask a question to further understand how the person thinks his or her solution is workable."

Teacher: Then, perhaps the nameless student might say something like, "Hanna, I don't think that idea would work because I don't see how we could list every number possible on the table—that would take forever." (This allows for the possibility that Hannah is two steps ahead of the nameless student and has already thought that part of the problem through.)

A special note about roles in groups: I believe in working toward eliminating these group roles as the students develop the ability to monitor themselves. In the real world, people do not assign themselves roles when engaging in discussions, so our goal is to support students in progressing to a natural manner of engaging in productive talk. For example, I ended up in a conversation in the hallway the other day with three colleagues about a work issue. We did not agree on roles for the discussion—we just began talking, with each person making an argument and others agreeing or disagreeing with the stated points.

I believe our ultimate goal with middle level students is to help them develop the skills necessary to engage in productive discussions with anyone, using evidence to support their claims. Ideally, discourse among citizens in our society should happen naturally and respectfully, without rules and structure to govern it. I understand this is an ideal and that many discussions are governed by rules and structure, such as those of Congress. But ideally, polite, respectful, thoughtful people should be able to discuss differences civilly without a moderator. Of course, middle level students will need more structure than adults, but our goal should be to gradually remove that structure so that conversations happen more naturally.

Another difficulty of assigning group roles is that they can limit students' contributions to only those of their assigned roles. For example, the person assigned to gather materials may think his work is done once he collects them unless he has explicit instructions to contribute to the problem solving of the group; the recorder may need explicit direction to realize she must record the ideas of the GROUP and that if she is confused, she should challenge the group to clarify exactly what they as a unit have decided (if she can't articulate it, then the group may not have reached true consensus). You want to choose the roles carefully and explain clearly that all students are responsible for contributing ideas and learning the material, regardless of their assigned roles.

Pacing: Finally, my most important advice for helping students successfully work in small groups is to use a timer. Clearly display the timer so that students can see it and can pace themselves. The students need to be able to see how much discussion time is left for them to accomplish the task. Most groups of middle level students are going to need small amounts of time to pace, usually 10 minutes or less. For example, if you want them to (1) spend time brainstorming, (2) spend time evaluating their ideas, (3) agree on one solution as a group, and (4) finalize their poster, break that up into segments. Set the timer for 5 minutes, and give them 5 minutes to brainstorm. Then set the timer for 10 minutes and tell them to evaluate their ideas and agree upon one group solution or answer by the end of the 10 minutes. Then set the timer for 5 minutes and have them explain their group idea on their poster. As your students get better at pacing, you may be able to give them longer periods of time to pace themselves as the year progresses, but keep in mind the 10-15 minute rule from Chapter 4 and never give them more than 15 minutes for a task. Of course, the amount of time you set depends on the complexity of the question or task. Commercial timers are available for purchase or you can use free websites such as online-stopwatch.com

Role of the teacher: So, what is the teacher doing while the groups are discussing? A lot. You probably guessed that I wasn't going to say prop your feet up and sip a latte, right? First, you need to actively monitor all of the groups. Continuously walk around the room. Sometimes it is helpful to sit down with a group and get on eye level with them to listen to them or to ask questions. But sitting down at your desk is definitely not an option. As you are walking around, listen to the ideas of the students. Look at the lists they have created. See what strategies they are using to solve the problem. Determine whether groups need support through your facilitating the delegation of tasks, resolving conflicts, or encouraging them by positive reinforcement. Start forming a plan for which group should present first. It is often preferable for the lowest-level ideas to be presented first, and then move to more creative or thought-provoking ones. Additionally, while you are monitoring the groups, assess their progress on the Comprehension and Collaboration Standards. Helpful ideas of how to do this is provided in Chapter 10.

Chapter 8
Small Group Structures for Discussions

The strategies in Chapter 5 were methods to facilitate a whole class discussing one question at one time. This chapter changes the focus to small groups discussing a question and then moving to whole class discussions of the same question. I have found that just telling middle school students to get into small groups and talk about a question does not produce higher level thinking and deep discussions. Having a variety of ways to structure those discussions brings excitement into the classroom and increases the level of engagement of the students. An added benefit of beginning a discussion in small groups is that students can organize and refine their thoughts before sharing them publicly with the whole class. Teachers can use the various small group strategies in this chapter to teach a wide range of skills, standards, subjects, and grade levels. For the templates of cards with these strategies to use on a ring binder, go to Appendix E and amle.org/GettingThemtoTalk.

Carousel

Overview

The Carousel strategy (Spencer, 2008) gets students up and moving and allows for exploration of more than one question at a time. It is named after the carousel at the fair because students circle around the room, stopping to make comments on posters as they go. An additional benefit to this strategy is that it requires students to add thoughts to what previous students said, so they will go beyond the surface-level response.

Step-by-Step

1. The teacher posts chart paper around the room. Each piece of chart paper has one open-ended question written in black marker at the top.

2. Students are assigned to small groups. Each group gets a different colored marker.

3. Each group rotates through the posters and makes a different comment than the groups before them.

4. Once all the groups have rotated through all of the posters, the teacher leads a whole class discussion based on the ideas from the posters.

Tips

1. The number of posters needs to match the number of groups.

2. Use a timer to signal the groups when it is time to move to the next poster.

3. Allow the students to take their books and/or notes with them.

4. The whole class discussion at the end is the critical piece of this process. It gives the teacher the opportunity to pull together the key ideas he or she wants to address. The carousel portion helps students form their thoughts.

6-3-1

Overview

This strategy helps students begin to make sense of and organize their thoughts about what they have read. It helps them to narrow down all of the information in a text to a few salient points and requires them to consider the points that their classmates thought were important.

Step-By-Step

1. The teacher instructs the students to individually write down the six most important concepts from the reading.

2. The students are arranged into groups of three. Each group narrows down all 3 lists to the three most important concepts from the reading.

3. For the whole class discussion, each group shares one idea from their group list.

Tips

1. As the groups are presenting their one idea, have someone type those ideas into a computer that is being projected on the screen.

2. Another possibility is to have the students write their one idea on a piece of paper that is projected on the document camera for the whole class to see, or the ideas can simply be written on the board.

3. Require the class to take notes of the ideas shared both in their group discussions and the whole class discussion.

4. Have your own list ready, so that you can give ideas that were not shared by the students, yet you believe are important concepts.

5. The whole class discussion at the end is the critical piece of this process. It gives the teacher the opportunity to pull together the key ideas he or she wants to address. The 6-3-1 portion helps students form their thoughts.

Word Sort

Overview

The Word Sort (Spencer, 2008) is a good strategy for focusing on vocabulary, but it also focuses on key ideas in a reading as well. It requires students to not only identify key terms, but to also categorize them. This involves a higher level of thinking and will get your students engaged with a little more depth.

Step-By-Step

1. Each student writes 10 words that were important in the reading on small cards.

2. Students get into small groups.

3. Each group sorts the words from all of the members into 3-4 categories.

4. Each group chooses the 5 most important words.

5. Each group writes one sentence using those 5 words.

6. For the whole class discussion have the groups share their sentences and discuss whether they agree or disagree with the statements they have made.

Tips

1. Display the steps one at a time. Do not allow the students to circumvent the process or be tempted to skip steps by displaying the whole list at one time.

2. Give the students cards and markers to write one word on each card. This makes the sorting easier because it is easier for every group member to read all of the words.

3. As the groups are sharing their sentences, have someone type those sentences into the computer that is being projected on the screen.

4. Another possibility is to have the students write their sentence on a piece of paper that is projected on the document camera for the whole class to see, or the sentences can simply be written on the board.

5. The whole class discussion at the end is the critical piece of this process. It gives the teacher the opportunity to pull together the key ideas he or she wants to address. The word sort portion helps students form their thoughts.

Student Led Questioning

Overview

This is a great strategy for helping students begin to take ownership of their learning. Participating in discussions is important for students, but having them actually lead discussions takes it a step further.

Step-By-Step

1. Each student in the group has a different question on a slip of paper.
2. Each student leads the small group discussion of their question.
3. During the whole class discussion the students who had each question report what their group discussed.

Tips

1. The number of questions needs to equal the number of students in each group. In other words, if there are 4 students per group, then each group will be discussing the same 4 questions as the rest of the groups in the class.
2. Help students pace themselves by using a timer, which is displayed for all to see. For example, if you want them to spend about 2 minutes per question and there are 4 questions, set the timer for 9 minutes. Every 2 minutes tell the students they need to begin the next question if they haven't already.
3. Discuss the questions one at a time during the whole class discussion. In other words, talk about the responses from all of the groups to Question 1 before moving on to Question 2.
4. The whole class discussion at the end is the critical piece of this process. It gives the teacher the opportunity to pull together the key ideas he or she wants to address. The student led questioning portion helps students form their thoughts.

Bone to Pick with You

Overview

The bone to pick with you strategy encourages students to "gnaw on" a question for a while in small groups and then share their ideas with the class.

Step-By-Step

1. The teacher develops several discussion questions related to the topic and writes each on a cutout of a dog bone.

2. Each group selects a bone from the pile to gnaw on.

3. When the group believes they have gnawed the bone clean, they share their response with the class.

4. Students in other groups should add to what the presenting group shares. You can ask them whether they agree or disagree and the reasons for their positions.

Tips

1. The number of questions could equal the number of groups. Or you could choose to have several groups gnawing on the same question.

2. When a group is sharing what they discussed, display the question on the board for all of the groups to see.

3. The whole class discussion at the end is the critical piece of this process. It gives the teacher the opportunity to pull together the key ideas he or she wants to address. The bone portion helps students form their thoughts.

Numbered Heads Together

Overview

This strategy has built in accountability and requires groups to make sure every member of the group understands the group's response. It doesn't allow for any loafers or weak links. Everyone has to be ready to share.

Step-By-Step

1. Teams of four are established.

2. Each member of a team is given a number of 1, 2, 3, or 4.

3. A question is asked of the group. The group works together to answer the question so that all members can verbally answer the question.

4. The teacher calls out a number, for example-two, and the person who has been assigned two from each group is asked to give the answer on behalf of their group.

5. This leads into a whole class discussion of the question.

Tips

1. A quick way to establish the groups is to color-code the numbers. For example, you would have 4 red cards, each with a number (1-4) written on it. All the students that end up with a red card are grouped together. The four students with a blue number are together, and so forth.

2. Be sure to post the question on the board for all to see.

3. The whole class discussion at the end is the critical piece of this process. It gives the teacher the opportunity to pull together the key ideas he or she wants to address. The numbered heads portion helps students form their thoughts.

Jigsaw

Overview

The Jigsaw (Aronson, Blaney, Stephin, Sikes, & Snapp, 1978) is a tried-and-true group strategy that requires students to teach other students, thus learning the material in-depth. Students are arranged in expert groups and learn a portion of the topic in depth so that they can explain the material to their mixed groups.

Step-By-Step

1. Students are arranged into expert groups.
2. Each group becomes experts on a particular question.
3. Students are then rearranged into mixed groups, with one expert from each of the expert groups.
4. Each expert in the mixed group shares their question and expertise with the rest of the group.
5. This leads into a whole class discussion about the questions that were originally posed.

Tips

1. Assigning letters to the expert groups and numbers to the mixed groups makes it less confusing. For example, as a student I could receive the card A-1 as I walk in the door. That tells me that I am in expert group A and in mixed group 1.
2. If possible, check in with each expert group before you split them into mixed groups to ensure they really have become experts on their questions.
3. The whole class discussion at the end is the critical piece of this process. It gives the teacher the opportunity to pull together the key ideas he or she wants to address. The jigsaw portion helps students form their thoughts.

Elevator Talk

Overview

This strategy requires students to determine the most compelling pieces of evidence for their argument and to encapsulate their argument into a concise presentation.

Step-By-Step

1. Students are told that each group will have 2 minutes in the elevator with an influential person (governor, president, school board member, etc.).
2. Each group is to prepare the talking points that they will use to convince the person of their position.
3. The group needs to be clear on what actions they want the person to take.
4. The teacher plays the role of the designated official in the pretend elevator and each group gets in the elevator one at a time.
5. This leads into a whole class discussion where the class determines the most compelling evidence presented.

Tips

1. Use a timer for the elevator talks.
2. The whole class discussion at the end is the critical piece of this process. It gives the teacher the opportunity to pull together the key ideas he or she wants to address. The elevator portion helps students form their thoughts.

It is important with each of these strategies that you follow the small group discussion with the whole class discussion. There are several reasons for this. First, you cannot be with every small group all the time, and therefore have no way of knowing the quality of their discussions. You need to ensure that no misconceptions were formed and that they covered all of the important ideas. Second, the whole class discussion serves as a means of accountability and requires all of the small groups to be prepared to share their ideas with the whole class. This will help to keep students focused on the task at hand. Finally, it gives you the opportunity to pull all of their ideas together and highlight the key ideas that you want to address. Chapter 9 offers a variety of ways to organize those whole class discussions.

Chapter 9
Sharing the Talk

One of the most effective methods to get students engaged in rich discussions is to develop a clear purpose—if students are aware that the discussion outcome will be used in some way, they will be more motivated to discuss it at a deeper level and in a richer way. One obvious purpose is to learn the content well so that they can perform well on the upcoming chapter quiz. The only catch with this idea is that early adolescents are generally more concerned about who they are sitting with at lunch in 30 minutes rather than performing well on your chapter quiz on Friday. So, while it may be true that it is important to learn the material for a grade that will be earned later, a more immediate purpose will be more motivating to them. I suggest that requiring them to share what they discussed in some way gives them that immediate purpose. People, especially middle school students, do not like to "look dumb" in front of others, so they will work harder to prepare if they know they have to speak intelligently about something in 15 minutes. In this chapter we will discuss methods to have students share what they talked about, both informally and formally.

Another reason for students to share the result of their discussions is to develop presentation skills. Presenting ideas well in public is such an important life skill that it has been included in the Common Core Standards for middle grades.

Common Core Standards: Presentation of Knowledge and Ideas

- CCSS.ELA-Literacy.SL.6-8.4 Present claims and findings, sequencing ideas logically and using pertinent descriptions, facts, and details to accentuate main ideas or themes; use appropriate eye contact, adequate volume, and clear pronunciation.

- CCSS.ELA-Literacy.SL.6-8.5 Include multimedia components (e.g., graphics, images, music, sound) and visual displays in presentations to clarify information.

- CCSS.ELA-Literacy.SL.6-8.6 Adapt speech to a variety of contexts and tasks, demonstrating command of formal English when indicated or appropriate. (Common Core State Standards Initiative, 2013, Presentation of Knowledge and Ideas Section, para. 2).

Informal Sharing

We will make a distinction here between presenting ideas informally and formally. This section provides strategies for structuring an informal sharing of ideas with the whole class that were discussed in small group conversations. In other words, ways that we can synthesize all the different ideas that were shared across the room so that everyone is privy to all of the important points.

Poster (paper or digital)

In school, business, or social environments, group participants focus most easily in their discussions if they create a poster to share their thoughts first with each other and then with the entire class/department/committee. The groups record their ideas with markers on chart paper in response to the question so that they can present it at the end. Diagrams, graphics, tables, and math work is included as appropriate. Of course, this could also be done on a regular sheet of paper and placed on the document camera, or students could use Smart Tablets—or, if you happen to still have an overhead projector, you could give them a transparency sheet and an overhead pen.

In addition to keeping the students focused, this strategy makes the whole class discussion run more smoothly. As you monitor the groups' work, you can determine the order in which you want students to share their ideas. Sometimes, you might have only a couple groups with really strong ideas present to the whole class. If you keep the students arranged in the same groups for several days in a row, you can easily ensure different groups present on different days, giving everyone an opportunity to present. If you change your groups daily, carefully keep track of who is presenting so you avoid one or two students never being part of a presenting group.

Having the posters already prepared saves precious class time. You do not want a group standing at the board arguing over who is going to write on the board, writing slowly in their very best handwriting, erasing, and starting again while the rest of the class watches. If the posters are done in advance, the group can simply stand up and start sharing. I believe it is important for the whole group to stand and share their work. You may want them to come to the front of the room, or you may prefer to have them stand where they are if the rest of the class has a clear view of their poster. Have the students agree before they share which members will share which sections of the poster. This will create a smoother flow during the presentation.

Consider a couple more things. First, the responsibility for writing on the poster needs to move from one group member to the next each time there is a new question. The group members could rotate this responsibility if you have multiple questions within one class period, or they could rotate this responsibility from one day to the next if they remain in the same groups for several days in a row. Rotating the role of recorder keeps everyone involved in the thinking through of the answers (rather than one person always recording notes).

Also, students need to understand that anyone in the group could be asked to share the group's thinking. This keeps one person from taking on the role of "spokesman" and requires every member of the group to understand what the group discussed.

Class List

Another effective strategy as students informally share their ideas during the whole class discussion is to create a class list of ideas. The students begin creating a list of all the ideas that they can about the question while in their small groups. Every student in the group has a list in his or her notebook. Then, during the whole-class discussion, the students are responsible for adding new ideas to the list in their own notebook as they hear them mentioned. Creating a class list assists them with this. This list should be displayed somehow at the front of the room, so that students can easily get the list down in their notes. If you have a computer connected to a projector, you or a student can type this list. It could also be written on the board or document camera. Another possibility is to take whichever chart paper that was presented first, and just add to that list the ideas that were different.

However you choose to do it, establish the routine of having students share their ideas with the class. It should be the norm and students should expect that they will be called upon to share their group's work. This builds in accountability and helps students stay focused.

Formal Sharing

Establish times for students to share their ideas more formally in a presentation because it is an important skill for every middle level student to develop. This obviously can't be done in every discussion because it would be too time-consuming and you would not be able to cover all of your content. When students share their ideas formally, I suggest you give each small group a different question to discuss, which gives their presentation more significance because they know only their group is responsible for sharing this particular information with the class. I am guessing you are familiar with PowerPoint, the tried-and-true method, so I will share a few alternative technology tools that students have used with much success.

Prezi

Prezi.com is a free Web 2.0 tool that is an alternative to PowerPoint. While PowerPoint is linear, Prezi allows you to work with non-linear navigation on a map layout and allows for a creative format. It allows you to zoom in and out to show contextual relationships. It is right up the alley of middle graders. Serving the same purpose as PowerPoint, Prezi provides a visual aid for presentations and allows for the importation of the same things as PowerPoint: clip art, photos, videos, etc. But the presentation doesn't have to stay in the boxes of PowerPoint. So, if you wish for your students to do a more formal presentation of their answer to the discussion question you posed, you could ask them to create a Prezi to assist them in sharing their ideas. Creating a visual aid using a Prezi will help students to organize their thoughts and structure them before presenting them to the class.

Glogster

Glogster.com is a free Web 2.0 tool that allows you to create an electronic poster. There is also an edu version that allows you to purchase space that is password protected to filter out content inappropriate for the classroom. Students can import videos, clip art, graphics, photos, text, etc. into a poster format. This allows them to organize their thoughts in a visual display to assist them in sharing the ideas they discussed in their small groups with the whole class.

Voicethread

Voicethread.com is another free Web 2.0 tool that allows students to create a slide show in which they and others can add comments to the slides. The slides can be videos, text, pictures, Word documents, etc. The creator of the slides can make video, audio, or text comments about the slide. But when the link to the Voicethread is shared, others can add comments to the slides as well. In effect, the conversation that began with one small group sharing their ideas, can be extended electronically if so desired.

Haiku Deck

Haiku Deck (found at haikudeck.com) is a mobile app that allows you to create a visual display for a presentation quickly and easily. You simply enter a key word, and the application will search visual images that relate to that key word. The students can enter text that expands their ideas. Like the other applications mentioned above, this assists students in organizing and visually displaying their thoughts in an interesting way as they share them.

Educreations

Educreations (found at educreations.com) is a mobile app that allows you to create a teaching video. You begin with a whiteboard onto which students can import diagrams or pictures. As students explain their ideas, they can write or draw on the whiteboard or the diagrams to highlight important thoughts. The app captures this as a video tying the speaking together with what is written or drawn on the whiteboard.

These are examples of electronic tools that assist students in preparing interesting presentations. There are other applications and software available. The key is to allow students to use 21st century skills to develop and organize their ideas and to create visual displays that assist them in getting their points across to the class. I have found that students get more engaged on a deeper level with the discussion question and with the content if they are given the opportunity to be creative in how they share their conclusions with the class.

Structuring work time for formal presentations. If students prepare a more formal presentation using a technology tool, structure their work time. An effective technique is for students to discuss their ideas with paper and pencil first at their desks. They need to decide what ideas they want to share, what is important to include, and what can be excluded. Designate the amount of time for this. Then, designate the next section of time which students will use to create an outline or storyboard of the presentation. Use a timer to help them move at an appropriate pace. Once they have made all of these decisions, take them to the computer lab and let them put their ideas into the technology tool, again with a time limit. It is often helpful to have small groups of 2-3 students so that everyone can sit around the same computer and work together. However, some of these tools such as Prezi will allow students to work on the same Prezi simultaneously from different computers. Most middle school students are quickly comfortable with the technology applications, so creating something electronically doesn't take much more time than using markers and poster board. However, time limits are important so that students do not dawdle while perfecting their colors and graphics.

When groups present, it is important for all members of the group to be at the front of the room and for each member to play a part in the presentation. One technique I have used is to set a timer for 2 minutes just before beginning the whole class discussion. Have the students use that 2 minutes to decide who is going to share which part and in what order they will share. It is important for this to be decided ahead of time so that valuable class time is not wasted during the presentations.

Developing Presentation Skills

Public speaking is both a little frightening and a lot necessary for middle graders. It is an important life skill because speaking in groups is a regular part of the lives of most people—we speak in community forums, church and civic groups, neighborhood get-togethers, and work—and getting comfortable with it while in school is valuable. Most people are not natural presenters. They need to be taught the skills necessary to communicate their ideas effectively in a group setting. You want to set your students up for success, so teach these tips prior to the first presentation.

1. Know your topic. Learn the content first and worry about the presentation later. If you really know the information, the presentation will come together. If you don't have a lot to say, the best visual aid in the world will not make the presentation good.

2. Organize your points ahead of time. Think through what the main points are that you want to share. Decide in what order you will share them. Find examples or evidence for each point you will make. In other words, create an outline or storyboard of what you want to share.

3. Use key phrases about your topic. Select the top 3–4 points and have a phrase that helps you describe each point. Use those points to organize your presentation.

For example instead of:

> - When 2 blocks of earth suddenly slip past each other at a fault line, it causes an earthquake.
> - Scientists use recordings made on a seismograph at the surface of the earth to determine how large an earthquake is.
> - Scientists have tried to predict earthquakes, but none have been successful.
> - Scientists know that there will be more earthquakes in the future on any particular fault, but they don't know when.

Use key words instead:

> Causes of Earthquakes
> Measuring Earthquakes
> Predicting Earthquakes

4. Decide who is going to share which parts ahead of time. Nothing is more awkward than a group of students standing in front of the class debating over who is going to talk while everyone sits and watches. Decide ahead of time who is sharing what and the order in which they will share.

5. Use good communication skills. Speak slowly and clearly. Maintain eye contact with your audience. Speak loud enough for the people in the back of the room to hear you. Smile. Stand up straight and do not lean on furniture. Pause between ideas.

Helping your students develop their presentation skills is an important and worthwhile endeavor, even if it takes a little more class time. They will engage with the content at a much deeper level, which after all, is our goal. Help middle graders manage their time by giving them a designated amount of time to discuss their ideas in their groups. Then, bring the whole class together and give them a designated amount of time to create an outline of their key points back in their groups. Only after they have outlined their points do they go to the computer lab. If you start in the computer lab, they will spend their time selecting backgrounds and graphics instead of discussing the content. With guidance and structure you will be amazed at what your students can do.

Chapter 10
Assessing the Talk

Assessing discussion skills is as important as assessing any other part of instruction. To get accurate data on what your students can and cannot do in relation to the standards requires the use of a variety of assessment techniques. Ideally, you use this data to inform your instruction. This chapter will share some self-assessment, formative assessment, and summative assessment strategies for assessing your students' mastery of the Comprehension and Collaboration Standards:

- CCSS.ELA-Literacy.SL.6-8.1 Engage effectively in a range of collaborative discussions and issues, building on others' ideas and expressing their own clearly.

  - CCSS.ELA-Literacy.SL.6-8.1a Come to discussions prepared, having read or studied required material; explicitly draw on that preparation by referring to evidence on the topic, text, or issue to probe and reflect on ideas under discussion.

  - CCSS.ELA-Literacy.SL.6-8.1b Follow rules for collegial discussions, set specific goals and deadlines, and define individual roles as needed.

  - CCSS.ELA-Literacy.SL.6-8.1c Pose and respond to specific questions with elaboration and detail by making comments that contribute to the topic, text, or issue under discussion.

- CCSS.ELA-Literacy.SL.6-8.1d Review the key ideas expressed and demonstrate understanding of multiple perspectives through reflection and paraphrasing.

- CCSS.ELA-Literacy.SL.6-8.2 Interpret information presented in diverse media and formats (e.g., visually, quantitatively, orally) and explain how it contributes to a topic, text, or issue under study.

- CCSS.ELA-Literacy.SL.6-8.3 Delineate a speaker's argument and specific claims, distinguishing claims that are supported by reasons and evidence from claims that are not (Common Core State Standards Initiative, 2013, Comprehension and Collaboration Section, para. 1).

Go to amle.org/GettingThemtoTalk for the self inventory and all of the rubrics.

Self-Assessment

By assessing their group work students learn to recognize the comprehension and collaboration skills they must master and begin taking responsibility for their own development in these areas.

Ticket Out the Door

Middle level students are certainly capable of self-assessment using questions such as the following. Students could assess and be assessed by peers with such questions, and the teacher could also answer them, giving a third viewpoint on what was accomplished by the students.

- Did you read the text before the discussion?

- Did you complete your outline to prepare for the discussion?

- Did you use your outline during the discussion?

- Did you contribute ideas during the discussion?

- How well did you provide evidence for your statements?

- How well did you listen to the ideas of others during the discussion?

- Did you ask questions when you didn't understand?

- How cooperative were you during the discussion?

- What did you learn from the discussion?

- Did you enjoy participating in the discussion?

Obviously, answering all of these questions about every discussion would become tedious and waste precious class time. However, you might select one or two of the questions as an exit ticket out the door. Or have students respond in a journal. It's important to keep the rules of civil discourse front and center in their minds on a regular basis.

Self-Inventory

Another technique to consider for students who do not engage productively on a consistent basis is to give them the self-inventory in Figure 10-1. In a group setting ask students to read the inventory and think to themselves whether they might be displaying any of the characteristics. Have them do self-reflection, but do not ask them to share their thinking out loud. Another possibility is to pull an individual student aside and ask them to read the self-inventory. Ask them if they can identify with any of the characteristics. Discuss with them what you have observed and help them to develop plans to improve.

The inventory could also be useful at the beginning of the year or as a class activity with role-play or for students to do after a regular discussion that finishes early.

Figure 10-1

Student Self-Inventory

The Steamroller: Steamrollers tend to dominate the discussion and talk over other peoples' talking. Steamrollers know it all and can't wait to tell everyone what the right answer is. They don't listen well because they are planning what to say as soon as the other person finishes. You might be a steamroller if any of the following are true:

- I interrupt people.
- I find myself thinking about what I am going to say next and forget to listen.
- I say things that I later regret.
- I think I understand it better than other people in my group.
- I wish I were allowed to talk more.

Advice for Steamrollers: If you think you might be a steamroller, try counting to 10 before you share your idea and see if anyone else has something to say first. Another thing to try is giving yourself only 3 chances to speak during discussions. Once you use up those chances, be quiet and let others talk.

The Mouse: Mice rarely talk; perhaps they are afraid to talk because they are perfectionists and don't believe their contribution is good enough, or it could be due to shyness. You might be a mouse if any of the following are true:

- I don't like to talk in groups.
- I am not confident about what I think.
- My ideas are not very good.
- I get nervous talking in groups.

Advice for Mice: If you think you might be a mouse, write down ideas as you are reading. Before class, choose one of those ideas and be the first to raise your hand and share it. It is easier to talk at the beginning of a discussion than to jump in one that is already rolling.

Figure 10-1 *(continued)*

The Boxer: Always looking for a fight, boxers will argue about anything. Tending to make emotional rather than rational contributions, they are impulsive and generally talk before thinking. You might be a boxer if any of the following are true:

- People annoy me with their ideas.
- People make me mad when they say things I disagree with.
- I get upset easily.
- I feel strongly that I am right.
- I talk before I think.

Advice for Boxers: Try to really listen to what the other person is saying. Often arguments start when someone doesn't understand the other person's position and they jump to conclusions. Ask questions about what the other person is thinking before you give your opinion, and really think about the other person's perspective. Try saying back to them, "So, I think you are saying......is that what you meant?"

The Distractor: Typically off-topic, they are easily distracted and tend to distract others from the question at hand. You might be a distractor if any of the following are true:

- I get bored easily in discussions.
- I talk about things other than the schoolwork.
- I forget what we are supposed to be talking about.
- I like to talk about what I want to talk about.

Advice for Distractors: Write things down. Write down what you are thinking and what others are saying. Try to keep a list of as many ideas that are shared as possible. Keep the question the class is discussing in front of you and underline important words. Refer to the question often to see if you are answering all of the parts of it.

Small group self-assessment

Using a questionnaire with questions such as the ones found in Table 10-1 can be helpful. You can have every student complete the questions independently and then discuss their answers as a group and attempt to address issues themselves. You may also find it necessary to intervene with one or two groups and assist them in addressing the issues that they uncover.

Table 10-1

Group Self-Assessment Questionnaire
How well did your group stay on topic?
Is your group working well? Why or why not?
Did everyone have a chance to contribute ideas? If not, why not?
Is everyone satisfied with the answer that the group arrived at?

Table 10-2 provides another example of self-assessment in the form of a rubric, which students can study before the discussion to know what standards they will be held to. All students in a group as well as the teacher should complete the rubric and then discuss their answers.

Table 10-2

Group Self-Assessment Rubric

	Unsatisfactory	Satisfactory	Excellent
Pacing	• ran out of time before we had any ideas or an answer to the question	• had some good ideas to answer the question when the time was up	• had a well-developed answer to the question when time was up
Collaboration	• spent time arguing • some people did not listen to others	• everyone listened • asked questions to clarify • voted on best idea	• everyone listened • combined ideas to make new idea
Contributions	• not everyone contributed	• everyone contributed	• everyone contributed • gave each other support
Responsibility	• had trouble staying on task	• most people on task most of time	• focused the entire time • everyone tried to find evidence

As you monitor the groups while they work, you will likely notice students with a wide range of social skills. This information will prove invaluable as you plan goals for your future discussions.

Formative Assessment

While you are monitoring student discussion groups, assess their progress on the standards. An assessment technique that is useful for the Common Core Comprehension and Collaboration Standards is an observational checklist. You might break down the standards into sub skills and develop a checklist such as the one in Table 10-3. As you walk around and monitor the discussions, you can simply make tally marks when you observe a student performing one of the skills successfully. Collecting this data over several discussions will enable you to see patterns of strengths and weaknesses among your students and which skills you need to reteach.

Table 10-3: Observation Checklist Example

Student	Cites evidence	Follows rules for collegial discussions	asks questions	Builds on others' comments	supports claim with details
Aki	l		l		ll
DeShawn		ll		l	l
Molly	l	lll			
Sofia					
Nathan		ll		l	l
Santiago				l	l
Imani		l			lll
Charlene		l		ll	ll
James		l			l
Marguia		ll	l	l	l
Aran					
Isabella		ll			l
Ebony	l	l		l	

By looking at this example checklist, I can quickly see that referring to evidence from the text and posing questions are two skills I need to emphasize more and to spend time re-teaching. I can also quickly see that two students in particular, Sofia and Aran, need to be encouraged or supported in their collaboration and communication skills.

Summative Assessment

Summative assessment can be particularly challenging for the comprehension and collaboration standards because it is difficult for one teacher to lead a whole class discussion and assess students simultaneously. When students are in small groups, it is not possible to simultaneously observe all students and record the data. Therefore, it is important to collect data over time. Do not base your assessment of student mastery on these standards on one discussion. Consider performance in both small group and whole class discussions. I suggest breaking apart the rubric below and assessing students on one standard at a time.

Table 10-3: Comprehension and Collaboration Rubric

Standard	Below Standard
Builds on others' ideas and expresses his or her own clearly.	• shares ideas in a confusing manner • does not listen to others' ideas • sometimes interrupts to make his/her own point
Prepares for discussions; refers to evidence to probe and reflects on ideas under discussion.	• did not read the material. • does not refer to the text
Follows rules for collegial discussions decided by the class, sets goals and deadlines, and defines roles as needed.	• does not follow rules for discussions • interrupts • makes inappropriate statements • disrespects others
Poses and responds to questions with elaboration and detail by making comments that contribute to the topic, text, or issue under discussion.	• does not pose questions • does not use elaboration or detail • makes unrelated comments
Demonstrates understanding of multiple perspectives through reflection and paraphrasing.	• Is antagonistic towards perspectives of others
Interprets information presented in diverse media and formats and explains how it contributes to topic	• does not explain and connect to topic the information from diverse media
Delineates a speaker's argument and specific claims; distinguishes claims supported by reasons and evidence from claims that are not	• does not describe the speaker's argument • does not delineate which claims are supported by reasons and evidence

In Progress	Proficient
• sometimes clearly expresses ideas • listens as others share ideas, but does not build on them	• clearly expresses ideas • builds on the ideas of others
• unclear whether text was read • refers to the text—sometimes accurately • sometimes helps move discussion forward	• contributions show student has read and understood the material • uses evidence from the text to further the discussion
• sometimes breaks the rules for collegial discussions	• follows collegiality rules and discusses ideas respectfully with other students
• poses questions not related to the topic • rarely uses elaboration or detail • some contributions off topic and/ or not helpful	• poses questions related to the topic • uses elaboration and detail • contributions enhance the discussion
• tolerates other perspectives • does not demonstrate understanding of those perspectives	• reflects and paraphrases to demonstrate understanding of multiple perspectives
• demonstrates some understanding of information in diverse media • does not explain how its relation to the topic	• interprets and explains information from diverse media and formats • connects it to the topic
• describes the speaker's argument • does not accurately distinguish which claims are supported by reasons and evidence	• explains speaker's argument • distinguishes which claims are supported by reasons and evidence

Assessing the Presentation Standards

While the focus of this book has been on helping students to engage productively in class discussions, another set of standards are relevant. The Common Core Presentation of Knowledge and Idea Standards:

- CCSS.ELA-Literacy.SL.6-8.4 Present claims and findings, sequencing ideas logically and using pertinent descriptions, facts, and details to accentuate main ideas or themes; use appropriate eye contact, adequate volume, and clear pronunciation.

- CCSS.ELA-Literacy.SL.6-8.5 Include multimedia components (e.g., graphics, images, music, sound) and visual displays in presentations to clarify information.

- CCSS.ELA-Literacy.SL.6-8.6 Adapt speech to a variety of contexts and tasks, demonstrating command of formal English when indicated or appropriate. (Common Core State Standards Initiative, 2013, Presentation of Knowledge and Ideas Section, para. 2).

Students should have multiple opportunities to practice these standards and to demonstrate mastery of them. In contrast to the comprehension and collaboration standards, it is easier for a teacher to assess each student on the rubric (see Table 10-4) during a presentation, even if it is a group presentation, as you will only have one presentation happening at a time. If you use the same rubric each time you have students do formal presentations, it can serve as both formative and summative assessment. Students will hopefully see their progress over time. I find it helpful to underline the appropriate descriptors as I see them occurring during a presentation and supplement those descriptions with extra comments if necessary. However, extra comments often are not necessary, and you can just underline or highlight what you see during the presentation.

Conclusion

Using self-assessment, formative assessment, and summative assessment techniques is critical in helping students develop their communication, collaboration, and presentation skills. Students need clear feedback about what they need to do to improve and what skills they are performing well. As a teacher, you also need clear assessment data so that you can use that information to hone in on the skills your students need more practice. This information tells you what skills you need to re-teach and reinforce. It also gives you helpful feedback on the effectiveness of your teaching of these standards.

Table 10-4: Presentation Rubric

	Below Standard
CCSS.ELA-Literacy.SL.6-8.4 **Organization**	• main points not identifiable • confusing; difficult to follow • disorganized • lacks introduction and/or conclusion
CCSS.ELA-Literacy.SL.6-8.4 **Supporting Evidence**	• main points not supported by descriptions, facts, or details • many descriptions, facts, and/or details are not related to the main points
CCSS.ELA-Literacy.SL.6-8.4 **Delivery**	• presenter has back to audience while looking at visual aid • looked at notes too much • voice too soft • many words unclear • speaks too quickly or too slowly • missing or distracting hand gestures or body language
CCSS.ELA-Literacy.SL.6-8.5 **Visual Aids**	• no visual aid or visual aid does not contain any multimedia components
CCSS.ELA-Literacy.SL.6-8.6 **Language**	• no use of formal English • errors in grammar, spelling and/or punctuation make it difficult to understand the speaker or the visual aid

In Progress	Proficient
• some main points difficult to distinguish • main points not in a logical sequence • needs more structure • has introduction and conclusion	• main points clearly identified • main points sequenced logically • well-organized; easy to follow • effective introduction and conclusion
• main points supported by some descriptions, facts, details • most supporting evidence tied to main ideas; some evidence is superfluous • more supporting evidence needed for some main points	• main points supported by descriptions, key facts, details • supporting evidence clarifies, not distracts, from main points • supporting evidence convinces the audience of main points
• presenter looked at notes or visual aid too much • voice a bit too loud or too soft • most words pronounced clearly • some parts rush or drag • uses minimal hand gestures and body language	• maintains appropriate eye contact with all of the audience; only glances at notes or visual aid • everyone can hear voice • words are pronounced clearly • not too fast or slow • speaks with poise and confidence • uses natural gestures and body movements
• uses visual aid(s) with multimedia component • multimedia component(s) sometimes distract	• well-produced visual aid(s) support presentation • visual aid(s) have professional, engaging look • visual aid(s) clarify the information being presented • multimedia components are included • multimedia components enhance rather than distract
• multiple errors in spoken English • visual aid(s) contain errors in grammar, spelling, or punctuation	• demonstrates command of formal English • few minor errors in spoken grammar or syntax • visual aid(s) contain no grammar, spelling, or punctuation errors

Appendix A

Revised Bloom's Taxonomy

Revised Bloom's Taxonomy (Anderson & Krathwohl, 2001) consists of six levels of mental skills or abilities that are arranged in a hierarchy with *remembering* tasks requiring the lowest level of thinking and doing and *creating* tasks requiring the highest level of thinking and doing. All students can function at all levels of the taxonomy if the content students are studying is at the appropriate reading and operational levels of the students.

To some extent, one must be able to function at each level before moving to the next level, and practicing more complex skills often encourages mastery of simpler ones. Suggested verbs are associated with each level of the taxonomy, which can serve as a guide in selecting appropriate verbs for small group and whole class discussion questions.

Bloom's Taxonomy of Critical Thought

Remembering: Retrieving, recognizing. Sample verbs: Acquire, define, find, follow directions, identify, know, label, list, match, memorize, name, quote, read, record, select, state, write.

Understanding: Constructing meaning. Sample verbs: Account for, classify, compare, demonstrate, differentiate, explain, give examples, state in own words, group, illustrate, infer, interpret, outline, paraphrase, predict, recognize, represent, retell, show, simplify, summarize.

Applying: Using information. Sample verbs: Apply, compute, construct, convert, demonstrate, derive, develop, discover, discuss, examine, execute, experiment, generalize, implement, interview, investigate, model, participate, perform, plan, prepare, produce, prove, solve, utilize.

Analyzing: Break the information down into its component parts; determine how the parts relate to one another and to an overall structure or purpose. Sample verbs: Analyze, categorize, classify, compare, contrast, criticize debate, determine, diagram, differentiate, discover, discriminate, draw conclusions, examine, generalize, infer, illustrate, organize, relate, search.

Evaluating: Make judgments based on criteria and standards. Sample verbs: argue, award, check, critiques, defend, interpret, judge, measure, select, set standards, test, verify.

Creating: Combine elements to form a coherent or functional whole. Sample verbs: Arrange, combine, blend, create, deduce, devise, generate, organize, plan, present, produce, rearrange, reorganize, rewrite, synthesize.

Based on *Authentic Assessment: Active, Engaging Product and Performance Measures* by Sandra Schurr, 2012, AMLE.

Appendix B

Encouraging Students to Engage in Class Discussions

I reprinted parts of a classic Middle School Journal *article (May 1998) called "Encouraging Math Talk in the Classroom" because it is packed with great examples and models of setting up a positive environment for class discussions, handling false starts and misconceptions in empathic and productive ways, encouraging student interactions with each other that take the responsibility for clarification from the teacher to the students, and training students to work in small groups. Each time I read it, I learn something new.*

Structuring the Classroom Environment

Setting up a classroom environment that encourages math talk requires special attention—it doesn't just happen—at least, not until the environment supports it. The types of thinking tha become the basis for math talk need to be valued. The teacher can communicate the importance of thinking and communicating by creating posters that say:

- Pursue your hunch
- Share your strategy
- Experiment
- Justify
- Defend our ideas
- Verify your results
- Listen to others

To overcome student fear that their answers will be wrong or that other student will not listen respectfully, the teacher must work to build trust. In the following segment of whole class talk, the teacher reinforces a student's efforts to explain. The topic is prime numbers and the teacher has just asked a student to explain what a prime number is.

> *Bret:* A number divisible by one and itself.
> *Teacher:* Only evenly divisible by one and itself. And we had some questions. Some people doubt that two belongs on that list. How many people think it does and, if so, why?
> *Karrie:* Because you multiply it so by one, but, well, it's hard to explain, really.
> *Teacher:* I think you've done a pretty good job.

The teacher then called on another student who had her hand up. That student and others expanded the explanation Karrie was having difficulty expressing.

False starts are critical. The classroom environment must allow students to make false starts. A comment such as "We will help you" often helps a reluctant student to be willing to talk in front of the class. Teachers must model the behavior that is expected from the students such as attentively following a student's opinions (no put-downs). Encourage risk taking, and help students recognize that there is more than one way to solve a problem—and the "best way" is the one that is most meaningful to the learner. Applaud perseverance when problem solving and applaud the students' efforts at critical thinking.

Process is important. Critical thinking must be valued if students are going to participate in good discussions. Answers to problems usually require only a few words. On the other hand, how you arrived at the answer or why you think the answer is or is not correct require true communication. Try to convince students that critical thinking is as important as the correctness of the answer. The teacher can do this by praising the depth of a student's thinking and reasoning even if the answer turns out to be wrong. In the following segment of class talk, Steve has been explaining his theory about how to decide if a number is prime and has been unsuccessful in showing that it always works.

> *Teacher:* Okay. So, it looks like we're just going to have to keep dividing. Well, what can we do with Steve's theory? It doesn't work every time, unfortunately; but it was a great idea. Can we modify it in some way? Could we put some limitations on it so it would work? Could we make it work a certain percentage of the time, so at least it would help us decide if a number is prime or composite? What can we do? Terry?
>
> *Terry:* Well, I think it's true if the number on the right hand side, like the number on the right is greater than the number on the left. Because there's sort of a pattern going and if the number on the right is greater, then it seems like it's...
>
> *Teacher:* Okay, come show us. If Steve could just step aside for just a moment. Come show us what you mean.

Discussing an incorrect idea. Sometimes discussion of an incorrect idea leads the class in a new direction. As the teacher works at building a classroom environment in which students are willing to risk being wrong, students begin to realize that their ideas are valued, that there is more than one correct way to solve a math problem, and that their feelings will be respected by the teacher and other students.

Justifying solutions. Students need frequent opportunities to explain their mathematical thinking and justify their solutions. Teachers bring this about by asking questions such as Why do you think so? Does everyone agree with our answer? Why or why not? The teacher must listen patiently to a student's ideas and expect the other students to do likewise. One way to encourage students to listen is to have them put into their own words what someone else has said. Restating someone else's idea also begins the process of taking possession of the idea for themselves. It pushes students to consider: What is the idea? Do I believe it?

Developing interpersonal skills. Setting class norms will help students develop interpersonal skills such as disagreeing in a polite way and not using put-downs. The following excerpt shows how students learn to disagree. Eric helps others understand why a procedure is incorrect and illustrates the role of critical thinking. The class is discussing this puzzle problem: Each of my daughters has as many daughters as sisters and the combined number of daughters and granddaughters is my age. I am between 50 and 70. How old am I?

Nadine has just proposed that you add 50 and 70 and divide by 2. This procedure has been identified as taking the average.

> *Teacher:* Are we looking for the average of the two ages the grandmother can be between? Interesting question. Eric?
> *Eric:* I'd like to challenge her on that.
> *Teacher:* Why don't you go up there to the front. (Eric goes to the front of the room.)
> *Eric:* My age is between 1 and 1000. If you add it up, 1001, and split it in half, you get 500.5 That's not how old I am.
> *Teacher:* Does that make anybody who averaged the two ages change his or her mind? (Students' hands go up.) Maybe the average isn't what you're looking for.
> *Eric:* My age is between the ages of 1 and 70.
> *Teacher:* You'd be 35. And he's not 35 either; but he is between 1 and 70. Wouldn't you agree? All right. Good point, I like that Eric. I like your reasoning.

As students listen to other students' presentations, the listeners also have the responsibility to ask for clarification, to relate the presenter's strategy to their own, and, in general, to make sense of the other students' explanations. Students also need guidance in learning how to work in front of the class. Introduce these skills in the fall and have students practice them throughout the year.

The Teacher's Role

The shift to increased student talk about math may require the teacher to acquire a new perspective on teaching. The teacher must focus more on students' construction of meaning than on delivering facts to be remembered by students. Student solutions and explanations must be valued, requiring class time to be allotted to discussions of how students arrived at a particular answer. Valuing student ideas helps the teacher develop the patience to listen to several solutions to a single problem. The teacher must be flexible in designing lessons because students' discussions may lead the class in a different direction from the original plan. Developing classroom procedures that allow for this flexibility is often the hardest part for the teacher.

The following discussion illustrates some of the subtle ways in which a teacher can build trust, accept divergent answers, and help students develop the language and concepts of math in whole class discussions. The discussion begins with the teacher asking students to use their own words to describe a factor. Her words and her wait time emphasize that she expects students to think.

> *Teacher:* Who knows what a factor is? Who can tell me what a factor is in his or her own words? Think about it. (pause) Maury, are you thinking? (pause) Okay, let's hear Linden's definition of a factor.
> *Linden:* The answer, um, that you get from a subtraction or multi— er, no I's not. It's a, a —it's a, a division problem? I forget. I need to think.

Linden is clearly not sure about his response. The teacher, however, ignores his insecurity and, below validates his efforts. Linden then responds by providing additional information. Linden's comment is again accepted without criticism and the teacher includes Terry in the discussion.

Teacher: So, it has something to do with one of the operations.

Linden: You know, like common factor or something like that.

Teacher: Uh huh. Okay, let's hear Terry's definition and maybe it will come back to you. You're in the neighborhood.

Terry interprets the teacher's response to Linden as an evaluation of is correctness and shows surprise. Ignoring Terry's surprise, the teacher repeat's Terry's words in a questioning tone, providing sufficient encouragement for Terry to expand his explanation.

Terry: He is? That's different than mine. I think that factors are a whole bunch of numbers.

Teacher: A whole bunch of numbers?

Terry: Well, they're like different numbers for the factors.

Teacher: Okay, that's a good beginning. Take it from there, Brian.

In the final comment above, the teacher's words and the tone of her voice suggested that the activity of describing a factor was the responsibility of the whole class. In the discussion that followed, the teacher returned to students who had responded after other students had given explanations. The teacher asked students if they wanted to change their definitions or how they would change their definitions which gave them the opportunity to practice restructuring their explanation. This emphasized again that the whole class was responsible for the definition.

Appendix C

Technology Tools to Support Student Presentations

Educreations
http://www.educreations.com/
Students can create video lessons.

Glogster
http://edu.glogster.com/
Students can create electronic posters.

Haiku Deck
http://www.haikudeck.com/
Students can create a visual presentation

Prezi
http://prezi.com/
Students can create a visual presentation to tell their story.

Spaaze
http://www.spaaze.com/home
Students can create a bulletin board where they post ideas, notes, pictures, videos, etc.

Voicethread
http://voicethread.com/
Students can create slide shows, add video, audio, or text comments, and then allow others to comment.

Appendix D
Digital Tools that Support Rich Class Discussions

Online Stopwatch

http://www.online-stopwatch.com/

Online Stopwatch is a free timer that you can display on the screen at the front of the room. This is a useful tool in helping students pace themselves.

Random Name Picker

http://www.classtools.net/

The Random Name Picker found at classtools.net allows you to enter a class list of names and will randomly bring the names up one at a time. This is a useful tool to ensure that you do not call on the same small group of students to regularly participate in class discussions.

List Selector

https://itunes.apple.com/us/app/list-selector/id556631984?mt=8

List Selector is a free mobile app that will allow you to enter a class list of names and randomly select them one at a time, or randomly assign them to groups.

Too Noisy

http://toonoisyapp.com/

Too Noisy is a free mobile app that will monitor the noise level in the classroom and will sound an alarm when it is too loud.

Classdojo

http://www.classdojo.com/

Classdojo is a free tool that allows teachers to assign points to icons that represent students or groups of students to reinforce appropriate discussion skills.

Group Maker

https://www.superteachertools.net/

Group Maker quickly assigns students into random groups. There is also a random name generator on the site that you can use to ensure you do not repeatedly call on the same students during class discussions.

Lost on the Moon

http://www.unionstation.org/pdf/Lost_on_the_Moon.pdf

Help students discover in a meaningful and lasting way the power of synergy in group work with this highly engaging activity. After working individually and in groups, students use the "right answers" from NASA about survival on the moon to compare the more effective way of problem solving.

"Nurturing Collaboration: 5 Strategies"

www.edutopia.org/blog/nurturing-collaboration-5-strategies-joshua-block

This blog entry by Joshua Block discusses facilitating collaboration, one of the many aspects of teaching that requires skillful planning, a high degree of awareness, and on-the-fly decision making and offers strategies for the unforeseen challenges that emerge.

Middle School Fishbowl Discussion

http://www.youtube.com/watch?v=RwxnBv-dNBI

A middle school teacher describes the strategy and compares it to a traditional classroom discussion with the teacher asking questions and directing the conversation. Students model the method and a real-life class participates in their first fishbowl as the teacher guides them in learning discussion skills.

Socratic Seminars

http://www.youtube.com/watch?v=9vviG8rPH9Y

Making a strong case for using Socratic Seminars, this video includes a middle school teacher and four middle school students sharing their thoughts on the value of this method of discussion. The video presents the basics of using the method as well as some modelling by an elementary, a middle school and a high school teacher—all of which would be useful for any teacher interested in improving class discussions.

Post-its: Little Notes for Big Discussions:

teachingchannel.org/videos/enhance-student-note-taking

This strategy is good for getting reluctant students to participate by helping them prepare for discussions. It honors their thinking and enriches the discussion by helping them remember what stood out to them—it helps them hold on to their thinking.

Appendix E

A Ring Binder of Strategies

My graduate students use ring binders of cards with the various strategies and the steps for each. They flip through them to ensure that they are using different strategies regularly and not getting in the habit of using the same ones over and over again. See the photo below for an example of a completed binder and the following page for a sample of a ring binder card. Go to amle.org/GettingThemtoTalk for all of the strategies formatted for a ring binder

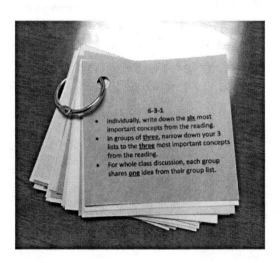

Sample Ring Binder Card

Speed Dating

- Pair students in two rows facing each other.
- First partner answers question for one minute, while 2nd partner listens.
- Second partner answers question for one minute, while 1st partner listens.
- First partners all slide down one seat to a new 2nd partner.
- Repeat process.

Adapted from Murphy, B. (2005). Need to get your students talking? Try speed dating! *The Teaching Professor, 19*(7), 1-4.

References

Allan, S. (1991). Ability-grouping research reviews: What do they say about grouping and the gifted? *Educational Leadership, 48*(6), 60–65.

Anderson, L.W., & Krathwohl, D. R. (Eds.). (2001). *A taxonomy for learning, teaching, and assessing: A revision of Bloom's Taxonomy of educational objectives.* Boston: Pearson Education Group.

Angelo, T.A., & Cross, K. P. (1993). *Classroom assessment techniques: A handbook for college teachers* (2nd ed.). San Francisco, CA: Jossey-Bass Publishers.

Apple, M., & Beane, J. (2007). *Democratic schools: Lessons in powerful education* (2nd ed.). Portsmouth, NH: Heinemann.

Aronson, E., Blaney, N., Stephin, C., Sikes, J., & Snapp, M. (1978). *The jigsaw classroom.* Beverly Hills, CA: Sage Publishing.

Beane, J. (2013). A common core of a different sort: Putting democracy at the center of the curriculum. *Middle School Journal, 44*(3), 6–14.

Brighton, K. (2007). *Coming of age: The education and development of young adolescents.* Westerville, OH: National Middle School Association.

Common Core State Standards Initiative. (2013). *English language arts standards.* Retrieved from http://www.corestandards.org/ELA-Literacy/SL/6.

Cooke, L., & Adams, V. (2003). Encouraging math talk in the classroom. In S. Schurr (Ed.), *How to improve discussion and questioning practices: Tools and techniques.* (pp. 9–13). Westerville, OH: National Middle School Association.

Dewey, J. (1897). My pedagogic creed. *School Journal, 54,* 77–80.

Gutek, G. (2004). *Philosophical and ideological voices in education.* Boston, MA: Pearson Education.

Hansen, R., & Hansen, K. (2010). What do employers really want? Top skills and values employers seek from job-seekers. *Quintessential Careers.* Retrieved from http://www.quintcareers.com/job_skills_values.html

Harris, B. (2011). *Battling boredom: 99 strategies to spark student engagement.* Larchmont, NY: Eye on Education.

Hollas, B. (2007). *Differentiating instruction in a whole-group setting.* Peterborough, NH: Crystal Springs Books.

Jensen, E. (2009). *Teaching with poverty in mind: What being poor does to kids' brains and what schools can do about it.* Alexandria, VA: ASCD.

Kagan, S., & Kagan, M. (2009). *Kagan cooperative learning.* San Clemente, CA: Kagan Publishing.

Lemov, D. (2010). *Teach like a champion: 49 techniques that put students on the path to college.* San Francisco: Jossey-Bass.

McCann, T., Johannessen, L., Kahn, E., & Flanagan, J. (2006). *Talking in class: Using discussion to enhance teaching and learning.* Urbana, IL: National Council of Teachers of English.

Mehan, H. (1979). *Learning lessons.* Cambridge, MA: Harvard University Press.

Murphy, B. (2005). Need to get your students talking? Try speed dating! *The Teaching Professor, 19*(7), 1–4.

National Center for Education Statistics (2011). *School survey on crime and safety.* Retrieved from http://nces.ed.gov/surveys/ssocs/

National Middle School Association (NMSA). (2010). *This we believe: Keys to educating young adolescents.* Westerville, OH: National Middle School Association.

Palmer, E. (2011). *Well spoken: Teaching speaking to all students.* Portland, ME: Stenhouse.

Schiro, M. (2008). *Curriculum theory: Conflicting visions and enduring concerns.* Los Angeles, CA: Sage.

Schurr, S. (2003). *How to improve discussion and questioning practices: Tools and techniques.* Westerville, OH: National Middle School Association.

Schurr, S. (2012). *Authentic assessment: Active, engaging product and performance measures.* Westerville, OH: Association for Middle Level Education.

Scott, (2003). Literature circles in the middle school classroom: Developing reading, responding, and responsibility. In S. Schurr (Ed.), *How to improve discussion and questioning practices: Tools and techniques* (pp. 14-19). Westerville, OH: National Middle School Association.

Silver, D. (2012). *Fall down 7 time get up 8: Teaching kids to succeed.* Thousand Oaks, CA; Westerville, OH: Corwin; Association for Middle Level Education.

Spencer, J. (2008). *Everyone's invited: Interactive strategies that engage young adolescents.* Westerville, OH: National Middle School Association.

Spencer, J. (2013). *Ten differentiation strategies for building Common Core literacy.* Westerville, OH: Association for Middle Level Education.

Stigler, J. & Hiebert, J. (1999). *The teaching gap.* New York: The Free Press.

Strahan, D., L'Esperance, M., & van Hoose, J. (2009). *Promoting harmony young adolescent development and classroom practices.* Westerville, OH: National Middle School Association.

Theobald, M. (2003). What students say about common teaching practices. In S. Schurr (Ed.), *How to improve discussion and questioning practices: Tools and techniques* (pp. 3–8). Westerville, OH: National Middle School Association.

Vygotsky, L. S. (1978). *Mind in Society.* London: Harvard University Press.

Vygotsky, L. (1980). *Mind in society: The development of higher psychological processes.* Cambridge: Harvard University Press.

Warren, L. (2002–2006). *Managing hot moments in the classroom.* Derek Bok Center. Retrieved from http://isites.harvard.edu/fs/html/icb.topic58474/hotmoments.html

Wilberding, E. (2014). *Teach like Socrates: Guiding Socratic dialogues & discussions in the classroom.* Waco, TX: Prufrock Press.

Wood, K. D., Roser, N. L., & Martinez, M. (2001). Collaborative literacy: Lessons learned from literature. *The Reading Teacher, 55*(2), 102–111.

Wood, T. (1998). Alternative patterns of communication in mathematics classes: Funneling or focusing? In H. Steinbring, M. Bussi, & A. Sierpinska (Eds.), *Language and communication in the mathematics classroom.* (pp. 167–78). Reston, VA: National Council of Teachers of Mathematics.

Wormeli, R. (2013). *The collected writings (so far) of Rick Wormeli: Crazy good stuff I've learned about teaching along the way.* Westerville, OH: Association for Middle Level Education.

CPSIA information can be obtained
at www.ICGtesting.com
Printed in the USA
FFOW05n1045100716

CPSIA information can be obtained
at www.ICGtesting.com
Printed in the USA
FFOW05n1045100716